3rd August 2018

GW01424125

A Short History of the Netherlands
From prehistory to the present day

His Majesty King Willem-Alexander and Her Majesty Queen Maxima, April 2013
© RVD

A Short History
of *the Netherlands*

From prehistory to the present day

Prof. dr. P.J. Rietbergen

BEKKING & BLITZ
PUBLISHERS

Contents

The Netherlands – a country won from the water
Polder mills at Kinderdijk in the province of Zuid–Holland

Introduction

The Netherlands as we now know it has gained its present territorial shape over an immensely long period of time, due to a variety of influences, both natural and cultural, including, of course, many developments of a political and military nature.

However, long before man had ever won or lost part of its territory through politics or war, he had experienced the gain and loss of land through the forces of nature. Indeed, in no other European country, nature, especially water, has played such an important part in the shaping of the land as in the Netherlands. As a result, from early times onwards the inhabitants have tried to devise ways to curb the inimical influences of water. The gap separating the men who first built mounds or 'terpen' along the coast of Friesland and Groningen more than two thousand years ago from the engineers of the recently completed Delta Project, is not so wide as perhaps it technologically seems. The need to control water always was foremost on the minds of the Dutch, then as it is now. What with global warming and the expected rise of the sea level, the Dutch, who, during the past decades, felt to finally have safeguarded their country, once more seriously need to consider their water management in the decades to come.

Water, however, besides posing many problems, also gave the Netherlands some of its greatest advantages. Situated on the coast of the North Sea, in the delta-region of such major European rivers as the Rhine and Waal, the Maas and the Scheldt, and facing the British Isles, the Netherlands has commanded the major transport routes of Western Europe for thousands of years.

Not surprisingly, therefore, its territory has been a bone of contention between many powers since people first arrived here. Consequently, successive foreign powers, as, e.g., the Romans, the Franks, the Burgundians and finally the Habsburgs and the Spaniards, have left their mark on the culture of the Netherlands. Because many battles were fought to gain possession of the country or to defend it against outside attack, the curiously erratic eastern and southern borders that still show on the map have been formed. They resulted from the chance front lines that were decided upon in the many treaties ending the numerous wars waged over the Netherlands.

This book proposes to first give a short survey of the country's past from prehistory till about 1450. The Burgundian-Habsburg period, up till c. 1550, having been a major formative influence, is described in greater detail, and includes the history of what is now Belgium, as that state, too, belonged to the onetime 'seventeen Netherlands'. The struggle for independence of the seven Northern Netherlands - basically the country as it is today - in the sixteenth and seventeenth centuries, is described extensively, as, during this period, the Netherlands were born as a sovereign state, a republic even, and experienced their first flowering, economically and culturally. This is followed by an analysis of the development of the Dutch Republic in the seventeenth and eighteenth century and the temporary loss of independence under French rule in the 1790's and the early years of the nineteenth century.

Finally, the history of the Netherlands during the past two centuries is recorded, beginning in 1813-1815, when independence was restored and the country was, rather surprisingly, re-established not as a republic but as a kingdom.

In this edition, the text has been revised wherever necessary, and new illustrations have been added.

P.J. Rietbergen, 2015
Radboud University, Nijmegen

Painting by G. Berckheyde (1638–1698) of the Amsterdam Town Hall on the Dam Square. Built in the 17th century by Jacob van Campen, it is presently used as one of the royal palaces

AM

1 Society, economy and culture during the prehistoric period: till 57 B.C

The Ice Ages

During the millions of years that, given the absence of written sources, we call 'prehistory', the consecutive 'ice ages' or glacial periods determined the character of Northern Europe. Yet, historical geography and paleobiology can help us understand what the world looked like in those distant eras.

About 200,000 years ago, part of the present Netherlands was covered with a thick layer of ice. This penultimate glacial period lasted till c. 130.000 B.C. The hilly ridges south and north of the great rivers were formed when moraine was forced upwards by the ice. During the following millennia, the polar caps started melting, the sea level rose and the valleys hollowed out between the hills by forceful glaciers filled with water. Consequently, although at that time the sea level was about the same as it is today, the coastline was totally different.

The ice did not reach the Netherlands again during the fourth and last ice age, which lasted until about 10,000 B.C. Yet, in that period the land was a desolate tundra, only. The sea level began to rise anew about 8000 B.C. Though by 5000 B.C., there were sea walls or dunes along what is now the coast of the North Sea, large areas of the western Netherlands were flooded regularly. Therefore, at the beginning of the Christian era, that part of the country was unfit for constant habitation, though nomadic people may have used it when circumstances allowed them to.

All that we now know of the earliest inhabitants of the Netherlands comes from archaeological finds, the product both of chance and, more recently, of systematic excavations. Thus, the 1996-decision to construct a major railroad through the Netherlands connecting the coastal region of Rotterdam with the German border offered a unique opportunity for research into early Dutch history. It now appears people lived on the site of the present Utrecht hills as long ago as 150,000 B.C. They hunted big game such as reindeer and gathered fruits and nuts. Their primitive tools were made of flint and included the famous stone axes. However, the growth of the icecap drove them away, and it seems it took a long time before humans returned. When they did, in about 9000 B.C., they probably had no permanent settlements as yet; quite likely, they still were nomads occasionally wandering into the region in search of food.

Thus, in North Brabant traces have been found of what may have been a campsite for huntsmen. The flint tools used by them were far more refined than those made by the earlier settlers. Axes dating from about 7000 B.C. were found in the North Sea, at that time a stretch of dry land, which only later was flooded again.

Whether these hunters, who also were gatherers, living on nuts and fruit as well, still roamed the Netherlands when new people arrived in about 6000 B.C., we do not know. We do know however that these new-comers were farmers, who probably also kept cattle. Perhaps they descended from groups who migrated westward from South-Eastern Europe or Central Asia, where, according to some theories, both agriculture and pastoralism had originated around 9000 B.C. It also is possible that these inventions themselves had spread westward, through some form of cultural communication.

Some of these settled groups - indeed, they probably were the very first people to settle here permanently - have been named 'Band Ceramists' because of the spiral designs on their pottery. They lived close together, in multi-family longhouses, and worked large farms, as testified by findings in the hilly south of Limburg, as well as on the high banks along the major rivers. Like their hunting forebears, they still used stone implements. Again in Limburg, flint mines have been discovered which must have been in use for over five centuries.

Megalith graves near Havelte, built by the people of the Funnel Beaker Culture
RMO Leiden

Statuette found near Willemstad, in Zeeland, dated c. 5300 B.C. It was carved from a piece of soft oak wood, probably by a hunter using a flint knife
RMO Leiden

The Funnel Beaker Culture and the Bell Beaker Culture

In addition to traces of their settlements and pottery, several of the burial places of the prehistoric inhabitants of the Netherlands can still be seen. Those left by another group, called the 'Funnel Beaker People', whose remains are datable to the period of c. 4400-2700 B.C., are particularly impressive; actually, they did not serve as graves, but as storage houses for the bones of the dead. These megalith tombs, or 'barrows', were built of huge boulders, first forced into this region by the ice; later, they were artificially arranged to form a vault, and originally covered with sand. The Funnel Beaker People were farmers and pastoralists, too, just like the inhabitants of the sea walls along the coast known as the 'Vlaardinger Civilization', whose houses have been discovered as well. They flourished between c. 3500 and 2500 B.C.; not surprisingly, fishing was an important part of their economy as well.

Traces of the so-called the 'Bell Beaker People', who may have evolved out of the Band Ceramist-group, show that they had achieved an even higher level of technology. Excavations have revealed they had mastered the technique of forging, using imported copper, which, of course, indicates the existence of long-distance trade that, by the same token, must have resulted in some cultural communication with the wider world of North-Western Europe. Actually, the Bell Beaker-civilization was one of the first to originate in the Netherlands, later spreading to other regions.

Also about this time, the first agricultural implements came into use, including the wooden plough. Originally, these would only draw a furrow in light soil, but they yet were a great improvement over tilling the land by hand or by stick. Soon, new agricultural techniques led to the increased production of corn, which in its turn enabled the population to grow.

Pottery belonging to the Funnel Beaker culture, excavated in the twentieth century
Drents Museum

The Bronze Age

The period between 1900 and 750 B.C. is known as Europe's Bronze Age because utensils made of copper and of bronze - an alloy of copper and tin - came into general use, marking another step forward in the field of technology.

This period also saw the start of widespread trading on an interregional scale, as can be witnessed from some remarkable archaeological finds. In 1881, a splendid bead necklace was excavated at Exloo, in Drenthe, made of tin mined in Cornwall, of amber - fossilized resin - imported from the Baltic and of earthenware beads from Egypt, brought here either by overland trading routes or by Mediterranean merchants; recently, however, recently it has been suggested that the glazed earthenware came from England, too, and that amber was found on Dutch beaches as well, showing that interpretations will continue to vary.

Funeral rites changed at the end of the Bronze Age, indicating a change in culture. The bodies of the dead no longer were buried but cremated, and urns containing the ashes were then put in special urn fields. Apparently, people now believed that the soul would survive, rather than the body. Funerary gifts buried with them suggest that in this period the inhabitants of the south of the country were of Celtic origin while those of the north belonged to the so-called Germanic peoples. Ultimately, however, they may all have descended from the tribes who originally had inhabited the vast region now known as South-Eastern Russia, Northern Iraq and Northern Iran. In periodic waves of migration, in the last millennia before the Christian era they trekked to India as well as to Central and Western Europe. This common origin, which is most obvious in the various European languages, has caused these people to be named 'Indo-Europeans'. It goes to show that, given enough time, anyone who arrives as a foreigner eventually will become indigenous.

A bronze funeral urn dating from c. 700 B.C., found near Oss. Besides the physical remains of a probably high-ranking person it contained a sword inlaid with gold, some bronze knives and pieces of cloth
RMO Leiden

The Iron Age

The production of iron, marking yet another technological development, has been testified in the Netherlands from about 750 B.C. At this time, also, colonists left the safety of the high, but relatively sterile sandy soil of Drenthe for the fertile sea clay of Groningen and Friesland. There, they, too, became cattle farmers, using the land for grazing. Given the regular flooding by the incoming sea, they built mounds on which to build their farmsteads. This seems to have been the earliest form of the Dutchmen's defence against the encroaching water. Not satisfied with safeguarding themselves in this way, only, in later years they also succeeded in restraining the water and reclaiming land from the sea through the construction of dikes, using pumps, windmills and other inventions to keep their land dry. Meanwhile, people continued to live, and prosper, on the dunes that stretched along the rivers, as testified by the huge royal tombs discovered near Oss, in Brabant, where bronze vessels and iron weapons with gold ornaments have been found.

Early 17th-century
painting depicting
the war between the
Batavians and the
Romans
RMA

In the final centuries of the prehistoric period, migrating groups coming in from the north of Europe succeeded in driving the Celts ever further to the south. Consequently, at the beginning of the period documented by written records, the present Netherlands were populated mainly by Germanic groups such as the Frisians in the north and the Batavians in the regions along the great rivers. The Roman author Tacitus, using data provided by soldiers who had marched north to extend the realm of the Romans, described the Germanic peoples as proud, touchy and warlike. According to him, unlike people in the south, who inhabited densely-built villages or cities, they preferred to keep a distance between their dwellings, built on their artificial hills. They sacrificed to their gods in wooden temples, or just in the open, on spots considered sacred nature.

2   Society, economy and culture during the period of Roman rule 57 B.C. – 406 A.D.

The first text mentioning the Netherlands dates from 57 B.C. It mainly deals with the country at present known as Belgium. In this year, the armies of the Roman general Gaius Julius Caesar defeated a number of Celtic tribes living south of the rivers Scheldt and Meuse, or Maas, such as the Eburons and the Menapians: groups who, at the very most, will have counted some 100.000 people. In his renowned *Commentarii de Bello Gallico* - the 'Comments on the War in Gaul' - Caesar describes the Celtic peoples in detail. This earliest written record of the Netherlands later was used by such authors as the Roman historian Tacitus who, in his *Germania*, of A.D. 98, described the civilization of the peoples living on both sides of the Empire's northern border. According to him, Celtic culture was quite splendid, as can be seen from archaeological finds, such as the richly-ornamented bronze mirror discovered at Nijmegen, or the beautiful silver vase from Neerharen village.

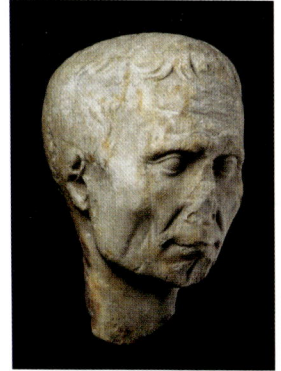

Marble head of Gaius Julius Caesar (100–44 B.C.), found near Nijmegen
RMO

The influence of Roman culture

The advent of the Romans had far-reaching consequences for the lifestyle of the native tribes. Caesar and his successors decided to establish the frontier of the Roman Empire along the Rhine, consolidating it with a series of strategic, well-defended garrison camps, connected by roads and, sometimes, canals, which enabled the swift move of armies and supplies as well as stimulating trade. Nijmegen was one of these camps. In addition to the infrastructural network the Romans created when they settled here permanently, they brought their culture - religion, language and everyday

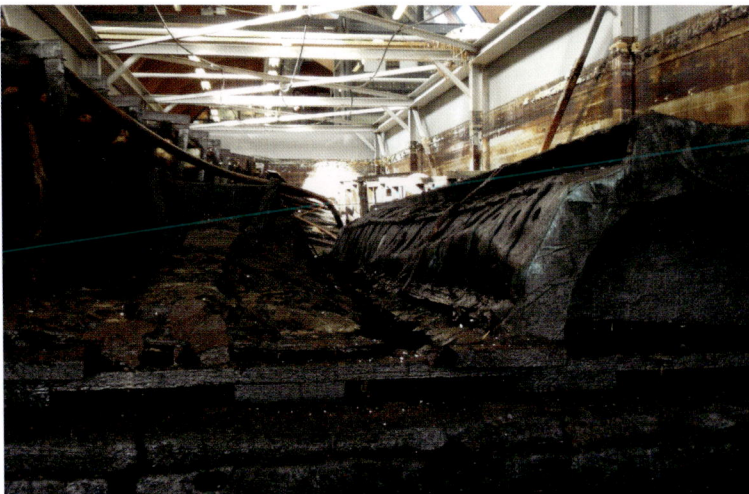

Remains of a Roman ship, found at Woerden, 2003

Roman helm masque,
bronze and gilt–silver,
1st century A.D., found
near Nijmegen

life - which now blended with Gallic and Germanic customs, in some cases supplanting these altogether.

Temples were built, such as the one found in the village of Elst, in the Betuwe, now buried beneath the local church - a sign of the way in which the later Christians celebrated their victory over the pagan religions. Beautiful villas were constructed as the centre of great farming estates, their rooms decorated with colourful frescoes and mosaics, and equipped with elaborate bathing facilities. Gold and silver jewellery and utensils were introduced. Moreover, the economy of the indigenous peoples, largely based on barter, now was influenced by the monetised system of the Romans.

All this mostly affected the Celtic-Germanic tribes living south of the great rivers. The Frisians who lived further north never were subjected to Roman rule although they were obliged to pay tribute for some time, till they shook off even this yoke during an uprising in A.D. 28. Yet the northern Netherlands were influenced by the Romans, too, through their trade with the garrison towns, which they supplied with corn and other foodstuffs, as well as with leather for shields and military clothing; in return, they would get luxury goods and, with these, a suggestion of a Roman life-style.

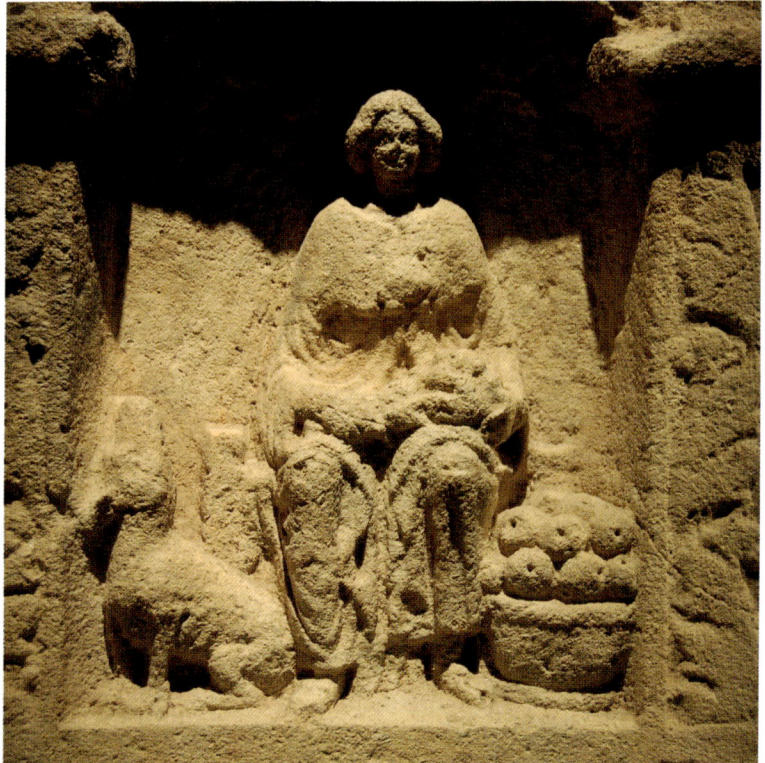

Altar of the Goddess
Nehalennia, ca 150–
250 A.D.

Artificial waterways

A few centuries earlier, native tribes had first built artificial barriers against the sea. Now the Romans set about constructing the first artificial waterways. One of the military commanders, Drusus, ordered a dam to be built near Cleves in 12 B.C., to ensure sufficient depth of the northern tributaries of the Rhine. He also had a canal dug to connect the so-called Old Rhine to the river Vecht. Near the Roman "castellum" built there, a 25-metres long ship has been found recently, complete with a carpenter's kit. Around A.D. 50, the Roman commander Corbulo constructed a canal to connect the mouths of the rivers Maas and Rhine. The object of all these operations was to improve the passage of the Romans to the northern parts of the Netherlands that had not been conquered, yet, as well as into Britain.

In the following centuries the water again defeated the inhabitants. The whole western part of the Netherlands became an almost uninhabitable peat bog that was regularly flooded by the sea. While at the beginning of the Christian era the region around the mouths of the Rhine and Maas was quite densely populated, by A.D. 300 it was practically deserted.

This decline was caused partly by the waning of Roman power and authority. The military commanders in the capital, continually contesting for dominion during the third century, often lacked the means to control the outposts of the empire. Thus, forced by problems in their heartland, the imperial troops gradually vacated the Netherlands.

This had some serious and long-term consequences. When the Romans had first arrived, efficient administrative units had been formed by dividing the area into two provinces, subdivided into "civitates", urban centres of regional government, defended by the legions who turned authority into power. Three centuries later, as central government proved increasingly less effective, the organization of labour necessary to keep all these waterworks properly functioning posed a real problem. In the end, the system simply failed. Also, the northern borders now became vulnerable to attack, mainly from Germanic tribes or war bands who, in successive waves of migration from Central and Eastern Europe, tried to cross the Roman borders into the more prosperous regions of the Empire.

According to tradition, Roman rule in the Netherlands finally came to an end in A.D. 406, when the legions left, or were forced to leave the series of forts they had constructed to defend the Rhine frontier.

A unique silver vase found at Neerharen in 1831. It is embellished with geometrical motives, partly of Celtic origin. On the bottom is an illegible text, in Greek and Latin letters
RMO Leiden

3 Society and economy in the Germanic world, up till c. 750

Much of the civilization of the Romans disappeared when they withdrew from these parts. Consequently, Gallo-Germanic culture once more took its place.

Economically speaking, Germanic society was rather more 'primitive' than Roman civilization, as it was based on agriculture, only, rather than on trade and the cultural communication that came with it. Politically, it was less complex, too, and administration definitely was less bureaucratic and hierarchic than it had been in Roman times. However, on the basis of family- and clan-structures slowly larger political-cultural units were built: the aforementioned tribes, sometimes called 'peoples' or even 'nations'. These mostly were governed by priests and by chieftains and, in times of trouble, by army leaders, the latter probably chosen from among the bravest men of the community.

In the course of the third and fourth century of the Christian era, small, Germanic, war bands and other groups slowly united, forming larger organizational entities, sometimes described as ethnicities, or tribes. Gradually, two groups emerged, the Saxons and the Franks, while, to the north, the Frisians maintained their position. During the following centuries, these more complex societies were divided into shires headed by a sheriff of the tribunal and an officer representing the chieftain, later usually termed king. From the sixth century onwards, these offices usually were held by one and the same person.

A Frankish 'fibula': a bronze clasp in the form of a bird, set with an almandine. This jewel belonged to a woman of the 5th century, living near Gennep
RMO

The Crown and the Estates

Germanic states and their form of kingship bore no resemblance to the institutions of the same name in our day and age. The Germanic kingdom was not a fixed entity, either in time or place. Kings were chosen at a meeting of the tribe's free and able-bodied men. Sometimes, kingship became the prerogative of members of a particular family, who might boast descent from a famous, heroic, or even semi-divine ancestor, but even so it existed by the grace of the people, only.

The main concern of the king was to harmonize the worlds of gods and men, co-operating with the priests, the druids. In time of war he usually led the army, though others were sometimes chosen to do so, if they showed greater military ability. A king had no say in internal affairs such as the local administration of justice. These were handled by the local communities themselves.

Socially, the Germanic peoples were divided into four estates: the nobility - not always hereditary, yet, but soon made up of men descending from those who had gained their landed property in reward for outstanding military exploits in the past; the thanes or free-born men; the freedmen and the serfs. Only the men belonging to the two upper estates were entitled to take part in the tribal meetings; these, however, were not convened regularly and should not be seen as some kind of predecessor of present-day parliaments.

The Saxons, the Frisians and the Franks

The Germanic Saxons lived in the east of the Netherlands, though the centre of their power lay beyond the great Dutch rivers, in what is now Germany. Therefore, even though their language has left traces in modern Dutch, as has their culture, mainly in the rural parts, they will not be dealt with, here.

The Frisians, Germanic too, were descendants of colonists who originally had left the barren sandy soil of Drenthe and had survived on their mounds in the water-logged north for centuries. During the Roman period, they had started engaging in trade, bartering their own produce, mostly cattle, hides and wool, in exchange for luxury goods, or occasionally for bullion. Soon, they were most famous for producing the so-called Frisian cloth, well-

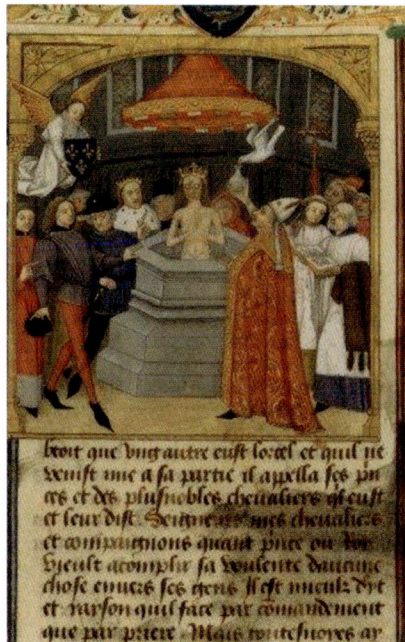

The baptism of King Clovis, as represented in a medieval French manuscript

known across the whole of north-western Europe; however, there is some doubt as to whether it was actually made from wool produced in Friesland, or bought by them in Flanders and then shipped and sold under their own name. By the fourth and fifth centuries of the Christian era, the mound dwellers had achieved a high standard of civilization in comparison with the inhabitants of the rest of the country. They were able to militarily expand their power and subsequently populate the southward region as far as the great rivers, even reaching Flanders by way of coastal shipping.

The Gallo-Germanic Franks who had settled south of the Rhine, Waal and Maas had conquered extensive territories during the centuries following the withdrawal of the Romans. From his base in present-day Belgium, Clovis, or Chlodwig I, the head of a Romanized tribe from the Merovingian dynasty and king of the Franks from A.D. 481-511, waged numerous wars to gain dominion over the whole of Roman Gaul, known to us today as France, and northern Italy. He also ruled over the Netherlands as far north as the Rhine, as testified by the Merovingian settlement found alongside the remains of the former Roman fortress at Nijmegen. After Clovis's death, his 'kingdom of the Franks' was divided among his four sons who, though expected to co-operate closely, inevitably fell out with one another. Theodoric I ruled the part that included the southern Netherlands, called Austrasia.

Meanwhile, the Frankish nobles, relying on their military might, challenged the authority of the kings and became increasingly independent. Especially the master of the royal household or chamberlain gained great power. From the seventh century onwards, this office became hereditary in the family of the Pippinnids, later called Carolingians; soon, they actually ruled the Frankish kingdom. Yet, like the kings, they too could not do without the support of the regional magnates.

The burial treasure of King Childeric (440-482 A.D.), one of the Merovingian rulers

4 Culture in the Germanic world: paganism and conversion to Christianity

The world of the Germanic gods

Archaeology as well as such descriptions as the ones left by Caesar and Tacitus show the Germanic peoples believed in the divine power of all natural forces. From their own everyday experience with nature's many incomprehensible manifestations, they created an imaginary world and filled it with gods who personified and hence controlled these forces. The mightiest of these was Wodan or Wotan, victor in battle and ancestor of all royal families: by extending their genealogies backwards to include these gods, the chieftains legitimized their authority. Another powerful god was Donar, who governed clouds and rain, thunder and lightning; these powers made him the most important deity of the farming community. Then there was Freya, the goddess of love and fertility. These and numerous minor deities, often locally different, were believed to influence everyday life for better or worse.

Being associated to nature, these gods were worshipped in nature, mostly at places which were awe-inspiring in themselves, for instance by a great old tree, or a source, or on a hilltop. Temples were built for them, constructed of wood. Sacrifices were made on an altar within a natural or artificial enclosure. Typically, tribal meetings were held there, too, giving decisions in matters political, which mostly meant military, a sacred legitimacy.

Conversion to Christianity under the Frankish rulers

Christianity, which had spread from the Near East over the Roman Empire during the second and third centuries A.D., already had gained some following in the Romanized parts of the Netherlands in the fourth century. Indeed, Christian cross signs have been found on Roman graves along the northern frontier. Also, a record states that Servatius, bishop of Tongeren, in present-day Belgium, took part in several meetings of regional bishops in A.D. 343 and 359. Servatius later moved his episcopal see from Tongeren to Maastricht, a former Roman camp town as well. According to legend he was buried where the great church that bears his name still stands today.

However, the real breakthrough for Christianity came with the baptism of the Frankish king Clovis I, at the beginning of the sixth century. According to legend, he pledged himself to the Christian God in the heat of battle against a Germanic enemy. Obviously, this baptism was politically motivated, to say the least. For Christians in the originally Roman towns and villages of the Frankish empire were numerous by now, and their efficient political-fiscal organization was a welcome vehicle to communicate the power and authority craved by the king.

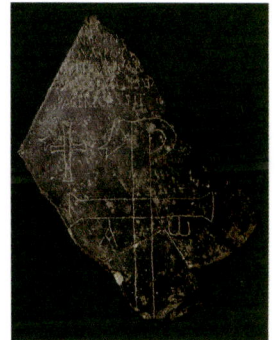

Early-Christian tombstone from the churchyard of the great basilica of St. Servatius at Maastricht, probably dating from the 5th century
RMO

A pilgrim sign – in this case a token that a person had visited the widely venerated shrine of St. Servatius at Maastricht

Strongly advocated by the Frankish rulers, conversion to Christianity of the entire region south of the great Dutch rivers was almost complete by A.D 700, but Germanic cults still were observed in the north. Although a small Christian church had been established at Utrecht in A.D. 630, the Frisians persisted in their ancestral beliefs. Possibly, they mistrusted the missionaries who came to convert them with the support of the Frankish rulers, viewing these men as advance troops of the enemy. Only when Christian preachers from Ireland and England, which had been Christianized already, came to work among the Frisians did conversion really take hold.

The first of these preachers was one Wilfred. Driven ashore on the Frisian coast while on his way to Rome, he was made welcome by King Aldgillis. He was able to preach the gospel in Friesland during the entire winter of A.D. 678.

Willibrord and Boniface

In A.D. 695, Pope Sergius I consecrated the Anglo-Saxon monk Willibrord bishop of the Frisians, at that time temporarily under Frankish rule. Willibrord took up residence in the old mission post at Utrecht where he built the churches of Saint Martin and Saint Salvator. However, he was obliged to withdraw from the town when the Frisian king Radbod drove out the Franks in A.D. 714.

After successful mission work in the German lands, another Anglo-Saxon monk, Boniface, though of advanced years, wanted to prove his worth with the hostile and headstrong Frisians. However, he was not willing to bring the gospel to Friesland until his colleague Willibrord had been allowed to return to Utrecht. This happened in 734, the year in which Friesland was finally annexed to the Frankish empire by the royal chamberlain Charles Martel. Yet not all Frisians welcomed Boniface's efforts. Thus, he met his end at murderers' hands, near Dokkum in A.D. 754. Indeed, despite new conversion campaigns, the old religions continued to flourish.

The murder of St. Boniface, in a 12th-century manuscript

SINT WILLIBRORDUS.

Fictive representation of Saint Willibrord (658–739 A.D.)

5 Society, politics, economy and culture in the Carolingian Empire, c. 650–850

The Frankish kingdom expands

For centuries, the great rivers had served as a natural boundary for the states of the south, first the Roman Empire and later the Frankish kingdom. The Romans had built a number of military forts along the Rhine. During the seventh century, around the remains of one of these, Fort Levefanum, a trading settlement developed called Dorestad, near the present city of Wijk-bij-Duurstede. Soon, this town became very important to both the Frisians and the Franks as it dominated trade in the whole of North West Europe: it was a central market on a route connecting the Frankish economy and the Mediterranean in the south with the Baltic Sea in the north. Through Baltic commercial relations with Russia, at Dorestad north-western Europe even was linked to the great Asian economy of the Islamic khalifs in Baghdad. Along this complex trade route, supplies of silver, essential to the economy of West Europe, came to Dorestad via Russia and Persia, while amber, furs and corn came from the Baltic shores, and wine from France; exotic products were imported from North Africa.

Inevitably, regional powers fought to possess this place. In 689, the Frankish royal chamberlain Pippin II defeated the Frisian king Radbod at Dorestad. After Pippin's death, Radbod succeeded in recovering the territory. But the rule of the Frisian kings was soon drawing to a close. As described above, in 734, the Frankish generalissimo Charles Martel defeated the Frisian military commander Bubo. Now, the Frankish kingdom was extended as far as the Lauwers-Sea and the North Sea.

From royal chamberlains to kings: the Carolingians

Charles's son Pippin III proclaimed himself king of the Franks after deposing the last Merovingian ruler. Moreover, he had himself anointed by the Anglo-Saxon missionary and bishop Boniface because he wanted to demonstrate that his kingship was of a different nature from that of the Germanic rulers, who were elected by the people or the nobles. Pippin consciously placed himself in the tradition of the Roman-imperial line and even more of the Jewish-Christian rulers, who always had been anointed by God's high priests. Thus, the Frankish monarchy gained a new dignity derived from imperial Rome and from Christian culture, with its Old Testament-traditions, as well as moving its power beyond the reach of people or nobles.

The Emperor Charlemagne (747/749–814)

Pippin III died in 768 and was succeeded by his two sons. The one, Carloman, died only three years later. The other, Charles, later known as Charlemagne, then became the sole ruler of the Franks. To defend and expand his kingdom, Charles 'the Great' campaigned relentlessly against the

The coronation of Charlemagne by Pope Leo, in a manuscript from the 15th century

Saxons, who threatened the north-west frontier of his realm. Following a decisive victory over them in 785, he had his rule accepted there. He also tried to establish his authority in the south-west, battling against the tribes of northern Spain, and the south-east, conquering parts of northern Italy.

Even more than his father, Charlemagne saw himself as the lawful successor to the Roman emperors whose rule and empire he wanted to re-establish. For this reason, in the year 800 he went to Rome, to be crowned there by the pope.

Yet, his empire had no fixed capital. Admittedly, Charlemagne often held court at his favourite town, the formerly Roman city of Aachen, but he also paid regular visits to the outposts of his territories. Thus, he sometimes stayed in the Netherlands, where he had a palace-castle at Nijmegen, another erstwhile Roman and, later Merovingian settlement that, moreover was strategically important as a border town.

The realm of Charlemagne was administered by civil servants, or counts, who were put in charge of the main administrative divisions, the counties. The names of several of these counties have survived in the present Netherlands, as Twente, "Batua", or Betuwe, the Gooi-region and Brabant. The main task of a Carolingian count was to keep the peace and administer justice, as the president of a tribunal made up of freemen, the so-called aldermen. In order to control these counts - who, due to defective communications in this vast empire, could easily become too independent -, the emperor sometimes used to send confidants to check on them.

The 'feudal system' as an instrument of administration

Though due to Charlemagne's conquests the Frankish empire was a vast state, especially in the times of the first Carolingians, the power of the ruler, of central authority, was definitely limited judged by present-day norms. Necessarily, rulers surrounded themselves with a number of trusted relatives and servants. Obviously, they could not personally govern the entire realm; nor could they base their administration on written orders, only: as most people were illiterate, authority had to be exercised

personally, and locally. Consequently, most princes had no other choice but to delegate the exercise of certain sovereign rights, in the field of justice and taxation but also in matters military, to regional magnates, the great landowners. These high 'officials' often were rewarded with even more land, as well as with specific privileges. Those who followed and helped them in their turn also were given land. However, officially these grants were not made to be freely held in perpetuity, but for a specific period, only. These 'fiefs' - hence: the 'feudal' system - were seen as the return for services to the Crown, which had to be rendered continually. The system, in so far as it was institutionalized at all, was flexible: even those who lost their land to a Frankish king in combat were then allowed to hold it in fee. In exchange, they had to acknowledge Frankish sovereignty.

The 'feudal system' and large-scale landownership

Agriculture still was the main source of livelihood in Carolingian times. But with the growth of the empire and the increasing power of regional noble families whose support was bought with favours by the monarchs, considerable changes in economic and social organization also occurred. Previously rare in Germanic societies, large-scale landownership now became the rule. This, in turn, seems to have resulted in a new class of people, the villains, who were granted a piece of land for their own use, but also were obliged to cultivate the land belonging to their local lord. The decline of a money-based economy, caused by the dwindling import of pre-

Farming in the Middle Ages

28

cious metal from the Mediterranean south and the Near East between the third and the seventh century, also played a part in this reversion to an agricultural economy. Payments now were usually made in kind or by means of personal services.

Trade flourishes

However, soon the increasing freedom and safety of long-distance communications guaranteed by the organizational structure of the Carolingian empire brought about economic changes. From the seventh century onward, besides agriculture, commerce became important once more. As the empire's boundaries moved to the north under continued Carolingian rule, this led to brisk trading in North-West Europe during the eighth and ninth centuries, bringing prosperity to the entire empire.

Here, the Frisians played a leading part. Precisely during this period, the trading centre of Dorestad became the foremost Frisian commercial centre. Over the past decades, archaeologists have been amazed to find the city far bigger, populous and wealthy than previously suspected.

However, during the ninth century, this flourishing community suffered from the devastating raids of warring adventurers from the so-called Norsemen, who came from Denmark and Scandinavia. Also, nature intervened: it is likely that the city's harbour was falling into disuse because the Rhine slowly shifted its bed once more.

Besides Dorestad, the towns of Medemblik and Stavoren developed into important commercial centres, too, as they were both situated on the shores of the great Almere - the later Zuiderzee, and now the IJsselmeer - and thus connected to the North Sea and international trade.

A Carolingian renaissance?

Charlemagne and his successors, as well as the mostly ecclesiastical intellectuals surrounding them, showed a marked interest in reviving ancient Roman and Greek culture, a phenomenon that has been rightly characterized as the Carolingian 'renaissance'. Charlemagne himself not only spoke and wrote Frankish, but Latin as well, and probably even knew some Greek. He also propagated the study of Latin amongst the elite. For written Latin was to be the 'lingua franca' of his empire and its administration, an efficient vehicle for communication. The Church took the lead in the education of the Frankish upper class. Inevitably, they put the curriculum on a Classical basis. The subjects taught were the so-called 'seven liberal arts'. The 'trivium', or triad, consisted of grammar, rhetoric and logic; it was taught to younger pupils. The 'quadrivium', the 'four subjects', taken by more advanced students, consisted of geometry, astronomy, arithmetic and music. Thus, during these times many a Classical text was saved for posterity by the zeal of learned monks. Indeed, monasteries became the centre of (learned) culture, keeping alive a tradition of Latin scholarship and of Roman-Christian civilization, mainly in the fields of philosophy, literature and the arts. However, most Church leaders only were interested in pre-

A gold, gem-set brooch, c. 800 A.D., found in Dorestad. It is inlaid with enamel, colored glass, semi-precious stones and small pearls, in such a way that not only two crosses are formed, but also, with gold thread, trees of life and birds, both referring to Paradise. The jewel obviously belonged to a church dignitary
RMO Leiden

One of Charlemagne's advisers, Alkuin, and one of his pupils present a text to the Bishop of Mainz

serving the ideas and artefacts of the Ancients insofar as these contained elements that could be used to create a well-educated elite to govern the Christian-Carolingian empire and contributed to a more civilized Christian way of life.

Obviously, education was the preserve of a select few, only: mainly prospective clergy and members of the nobility. It was provided at the court school at Aachen, as well as in monasteries and in the schools attached to cathedrals. The schools in Utrecht, belonging to the churches of Saint Martin and Saint Salvator, became renowned. From all over the northern parts of the Frankish empire, boys aspiring after a career in the Church were sent to be educated there. Often, in later life they not only would rule the possessions of monasteries and churches, but also serve as officials to the Carolingian kings and their successors, for they were, indeed, the only really educated group in Frankish society.

Charlemagne also stimulated musical education. He founded a choir school at Metz, and by adopting the so-called Gregorian plainsong he helped the clergy to introduce hymn-singing during church services, which, of course, made the liturgy both more festive and attractive. Such measures all strengthened the hold of Christianity over his people and, thereby, reinforced the cultural unity of his empire.

The division of the Carolingian empire

On his death in 814, Charlemagne, who had planned to give each of his three sons a part of his empire, and, thus, never envisaged a truly united, European state, was succeeded as emperor by his one surviving son Louis, nicknamed 'the Pious'. In 843, at the Treaty of Verdun, the empire was divided among Louis's three sons. Lothair inherited the central part - including the various counties whose territories later were to be known as the Netherlands - and the imperial crown.

On Lothair's death in 855, this central state was again divided, once more into three parts, with the Netherlands being apportioned to the northernmost part, the newly-created kingdom of Lorraine. Following various other divisions as well as subsequent annexations in East and West Frankenland, in 925, Henry I, king of Germany, succeeded in subjecting Lorraine, and the Netherlands' territories, to his rule. Officially, the entire region was to remain part of the huge, so-called Holy Roman Empire until the treaties of Munster and Osnabrück in 1648.

Actually, power over these territories and their many administrative subdivisions soon ceased to lay with the emperors and kings who succeeded the Carolingians, but now fell to regional magnates who increasingly showed their independence from central authority. Indeed, with the gradual weakening of central power in the centuries after Charlemagne's death, the major regional nobles became virtually independent princes.

One of the elements in this process was the chaos and insecurity caused by the invasions of the Norsemen or Vikings between c. 800 and c. 1000. Many people, finding the old rulers ineffective in safeguarding their lives and properties, now decided to entrust their land to powerful local men - whether these were lay landowners who were able to provide armed protection, or the rulers of the Church, especially the bishops and the abbots of the great monasteries, who had grown rich and powerful as well and could offer both military and spiritual security. Usually, in order to receive such protection, a person had to promise rendering military service to a 'liege lord' as well as giving up the formal ownership of his land, which, however, he was allowed to continue to use.

Map of the Carolingian Empire

6   The raids of the Norsemen, c. 850 – c. 1000

The names Norsemen or Vikings do not denote any specific ethnic group; they were given to inhabitants of the Nordic countries we now know as Denmark, Norway and Sweden, between about 850 and 1000. In the far, cold north, these peoples at best lived precariously on agriculture, fishery and hunting, and on what little trade they could get. However, as climate changes once more altered life in Europe in these centuries, and specifically jeopardized agricultural communities all over the northern part of the continent, their living conditions deteriorated. The Vikings now took to the sea, sometimes to find some honest and peaceful trade, but also to plunder. For a long time, they raided most of the European coastal area from their well-equipped longboats and returned home with stolen treasure. A silver necklace found in Scandinavia bears an inscription in runic letters which reads: 'We attacked the people of Frisia, and to us came the division of the spoils'. Thus they acquired their reputation as pirates and marauders.

Most of the Norsemen who raided the Netherlands hailed from Denmark. They regularly attacked these parts, especially after the death of Charlemagne, as central authority weakened in the Frankish empire due to the wars of succession and the subsequent divisions. Texts surviving from these years understandably blame the foreigners for all misery, even though the wars between indigenous princes and nobles caused almost as much damage.

The Vikings concentrated their raids on churches and monasteries: the only source of real riches, with treasuries containing gold, silver and precious stones. The worst attacks occurred between 879 and 882, when the Vikings set up fortified camps at various places from which they launched their forays. Their leader Godfried, the Pirate, even was appointed governor of Friesland after consenting to be baptized. He was not alone in conforming. During the first decades of their presence in the South, the Vikings attacked in summer only. Later they also took to spending the winter months in the regions they plundered.

In an attempt to limit the power of these marauders, the Carolingian rulers and their successors sometimes granted their leaders land in fee. In exchange, the Vikings who collaborated were obliged to assist the local ruler in his struggle against other Vikings. Thus, in 841, a Viking called

Harald acquired a 'princedom' on the island of Walcheren; a few years later one of his relatives, called Rorik, became ruler over the area that included Dorestad.

Declining prosperity. The end of the Viking raids

As all over Europe, in the Netherlands, too, most people were dependent on agriculture to survive. When nature did not collaborate - which now happened increasingly due to the 'little' Ice Age that occurred around 1000 A.D. - and when men, instead of working the fields, sowing, harvesting, and tending the dikes were forced to take part in military campaigns, the farms were unable to produce the food that was needed.

When the harvest failed in 892, a severe food shortage was the result. This was the signal for those Vikings who had not yet intermarried with the local population, to withdraw from these shores and to turn their attention to England; subsequently, only isolated attacks were made on the Netherlands. A modicum of safety returned, now. Indeed, the bishops of Utrecht, who had fled their town in the middle of the ninth century, returned to their see in 920.

The last raids of which we have documentary evidence were carried out between 1006 and 1007, when the town of Tiel was one of the places plundered. From this time onwards the Vikings were not considered enemies anymore, the more so as most of them had already embraced Christianity, and, with it, the culture of these parts.

Model of the castle at Borssele, as it may have looked in the 11th century. It is a so-called 'motte and bailey'- castle with a wooden keep to house the noble family and a courtyard for the stables, storerooms and the huts of the servants. This type of castle was normal in the Netherlands from the 11th century onwards
RMO

7 Society and politics after the disintegration of the Carolingian Empire: the beginning of regional sovereignty, c. 850–1350

Dirk III, Count of Holland (998–1039)

Dirk V, Count of Holland (1054–1091)

The development of territorial principalities

The territories that form the provinces of the present-day Netherlands really originated around the year 1000 A.D. After the incorporation of the lands of the Frisians, the Saxons and the northern Franks in Lorraine in 855 and in the German Empire in 925, slowly a number of large principalities emerged, mostly formed by conquest or by the merging of smaller counties, through marriage between the leading families. Most of these states were governed by hereditary counts or dukes. Though they had been little more than regional magnates who had collaborated with central, royal authority in Carolingian times, or had created their own power base precisely by using their office as senior civil servants, they all had gradually acquired both administrative power and extensive lands. Thus, by the tenth and eleventh century, they were largely independent, only in name subject to the German Emperor.

The counts of Holland

The County of Holland was the first to develop. The heart of this region was Kennemara or Kennemerland, which was granted in fee to the Viking Rorik in 862. Another Viking, Gerulf, who was Count of Kennemerland in 885, became the ancestor of a long line of counts of Holland. A century later, one of his descendants, Dirk II, was granted the entire region which he administered, between the rivers Maas and Vlie, in recognition of his support of the election of Otto II as King of the Romans, i.e. German emperor-elect.

Count Dirk III began to levy a toll from the merchant ships sailing in and out of the Meuse estuary, laden with profitable trade from both the North Sea and the prosperous heartland of Europe. A punitive expedition sent against him by the duke of Lower Lorraine and the bishop of Utrecht ended in failure as the troops floundered in the marshes surrounding his stronghold at Vlaardingen. This incident illustrates the growing independence of the region as a political and administrative entity.

The name Holland itself first appears in a deed dated 1083, in which Count Dirk V confirmed the property of the abbey of Egmond referring to himself as "Count of Holland". The subsequent Counts of Holland considerably extended their state in the course of the following two centuries, mainly by conquering territory belonging to their neighbours. For instance, Flanders was continuously attacked for the possession of Zeeland to the east of the Scheldt. This policy eventually was successful. Meanwhile, Zeeland to the west of the Scheldt was governed jointly by the dukes of Brabant and the counts of Holland, who, from William I onwards, were duly referred to as Count of Holland and Zeeland.

Holland also waged war on the Frisians, for the possession of West-Friesland. As the straits connecting the Almere to the North Sea grew steadily wider - due to the warming of the climate and the rising of the sea during the eleventh and twelfth centuries - the West-Frisians in their turn regularly raided and plundered Holland; increasingly isolated from Frisia proper, they still wanted to retain their independence. Indeed, this part of Friesland did not become part of Holland until 1289, when Count Floris V finally subdued the region.

Floris V

As Floris had been only two years old when his father William II died in 1256, a long struggle had ensued over the regency, weakening the authority of the count. But when Floris came of age and saw the potential of his inheritance, he soon showed anxious to extend his powers. The Kennemer peasants revolted against him in 1274 with the support of Gijsbrecht van A(e)mstel, a nobleman from the bishopric of Utrecht who himself felt irked by Floris's growing power. The dispute was settled in their favour, Floris being obliged to grant the peasants a number of privileges. After this they looked upon him as their great benefactor; he consequently was known as "God of the Churls". But his relations with such nobles as the A(e)mstels did not improve. Floris sometimes confiscated their possessions to punish them, only returning them in exchange for their oath of fealty. Both A(e)mstel and the lord of Woerden were thus treated. Finally, in 1296, some of the nobles took their revenge, capturing and imprisoning Floris in the castle of Muiden. When a group of peasants tried to free him, the nobles murdered him.

The struggle between Floris V and the local magnates was a sign of the times. In other Netherlands' principalities, too, a landed aristocracy had

The famous Count Floris V of Holland (1254 – 1296)

grown over-mighty, opposing the authority of the ancient rulers. As a result, sovereign princes increasingly joined forces with representatives of the towns that were becoming increasingly important both economically and, consequently, politically. Since nobles fought amongst themselves, too, town governments often received an appeal for help from them as well. Eagerly grasping this possibility to fish in troubled waters, urban elites extended their power.

The disputes between the so-called 'Hoeksen' (Hooks) and 'Kabeljauwsen' (Cods), two noble factions in the county of Holland, were notorious. They arose over the struggle for succession in the counties of Holland, Zeeland and Hainault, which had formed a personal union since the reign of Floris V. In 1345, the ruling count, William IV, was killed during a campaign to subdue Friesland. In the absence of a son and heir, the Holy Roman Emperor granted the three counties to his own wife Margaretha, sister of the late William. Her son William, still a minor, was appointed to eventually succeed her.

In the following years however, mother and son disputed each other's rights. William had persuaded some of the Holland nobles and a number of towns to take his side in the Kabeljauwse 'party'. The Empress Margaretha formed the Hoeksen 'party', with the support of other nobles. William finally gained possession of Holland and Zeeland in 1354, while Margaretha retained Hainault. But factional strife remained rife. After a few decades the feud between 'Hoeksen' and 'Kabeljauwsen' flared up again, once more over a matter of succession. But by then the independence enjoyed by the counties of Holland and Zeeland was coming to an end. A new, larger state was beginning to form in North-West Europe as the duchy of Burgundy, originally a possession of France, became independent and its rulers, by marriage, inheritance and conquest, acquired not only the county of Hainault but also many of the more northern states.

The diocese of Utrecht

Whereas Holland was a secular principality, the so-called 'Sticht' of Utrecht was an episcopal see, ruled by a religious leader, the bishop, who also wielded secular authority. Long before the year 1000, the bishops had been given estates and unused lands by the Carolingian kings, as an inducement to help them protect their northern frontier and to extend Frankish influence through the preaching of Christianity. From the second half of the tenth century onwards, the Holy Roman emperors granted the bishops the rights of a count, including jurisdiction in secular affairs. They felt this was the only way to govern an empire that, by then, had become too large and was difficult to keep together.

Thus, in Utrecht as elsewhere in Europe, the episcopal dignity, though a religious office, now evolved into a position of prime secular power, coveted by royal relations and members of the aristocracy. For instance, Ansfried, bishop of Utrecht from 995-1010, frequently fought at the king's side before his appointment to the Sticht. Only rarely were bishops clerics who really had a spiritual vocation.

Fictional portraits of Count William IV of Holland (1337–1345) and his sister, the Empress Margaretha (1345–1349)

In their subsequent struggle against the growing power of their vassals, such as the counts of Holland, the emperors sought added support by giving even more landed property to the bishops appointed by them, thus securing their loyalty. As the succession to a diocese could never be hereditary, the emperor would suggest to Rome one of his own favourites as the new bishop who, then, would be his faithful ally. Thus, in 1024 Bishop Adalbold was presented with the entire county of Drenthe by the emperor. In the following years, the Utrecht territory was extended further yet. The areas over which the bishops now wielded secular power were known as the 'Lower' Sticht (roughly the present-day Province of Utrecht) and the 'Upper' Sticht (the provinces of Overijssel and Drenthe).

In the eleventh century, the so-called 'Investiture Controversy' erupted between the pope and the emperor over the right to appoint bishops. Since the episcopacy was an elective office, and the right to appoint a bishop from a number of candidates was, at least nominally, a papal prerogative, Rome, trying to retain it, declared it would no longer allow the German emperors to actually appoint the senior clergy. At the Concordat of Worms in 1122 it was decided that in future bishops were to be elected by the canons, priests serving the cathedral of a diocese. In Utrecht they were organised in five chapters, led by the dean.

As the emperor lost his hold on Utrecht, the rulers of small neighbouring states such as the county of Holland and the county, later duchy of Brabant now tried to gain influence over the secular government of The Sticht. Whenever the See of Utrecht became vacant, they put forward the candidacy of their own relatives. Consequently, warlike feuds between parties supporting different candidates frequently divided the Sticht. In 1196, there were two candidates for the bishopric, one the uncle of the ruling count of Holland, the other a protégé of the count of Gelderland. In their zeal to acquire the coveted see for their own man, both groups occupied part of the Sticht. Peace was not restored until a neutral figure was appointed after both contestants had died.

Inevitably, the inhabitants both of Utrecht and of the Sticht at large were severely distressed by these military disputes that ravaged their land. Moreover, as candidates aspiring after the see needed a great deal of money to bribe the canons and then to defend their mostly precarious power, they often resorted to pawning their (future) property. In 1331, Bishop Jan van Diest was powerless to intervene when Holland and Gelderland divided his state between them, because he had pledged almost all his possessions as collateral to ensure his election.

Occasionally, the bishop was a strong figure and, like Jan van Arkel, from a powerful regional family, succeeded in reuniting The Sticht under his Episcopal rule. But even such exceptional men were unable to prevent the principality from being drawn into the influence of its increasingly powerful southern neighbour. Eventually Utrecht, like Holland, became part of the duchy of Burgundy.

Gospel Book, donated by Bishop Ansfried to his cathedral at Utrecht (c. 1005)

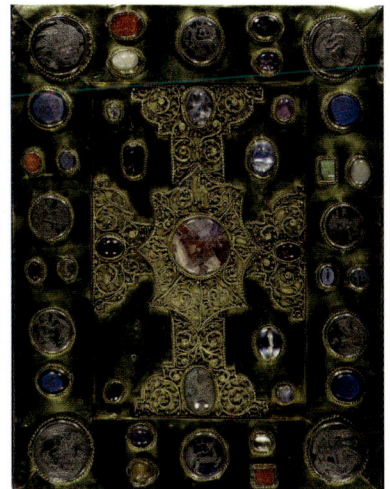

The county, later duchy of Gelre, or Gelderland

The county of Gelderland, which was raised to the rank of a duchy in 1339, was a late development. It did not begin to resemble the province of Gelderland as it is today until the end of the twelfth century. It did not even have a fixed capital. The dukes travelled around, alternatively residing at Arnhem, Nijmegen or Zutphen.

Like Holland and The Sticht, Gelderland was not spared aristocratic feuding, either. There, too, both nobles and towns fought for greater influence and independence. There, too, these feuds often sprang up over a disputed succession. In 1343, the families of the Lords of Heeckeren and Bronckhorst interfered with the regency of the heir, a minor, to the first Duke of Gelderland, Reynold II. From 1350 onwards they also joined in the feud between Reynold III and his brother Edward, until both rivals died in 1371. For many years the 'parties' of the Heeckerens and the Bronckhorsts to continued to compete for power, as did the Hoekse and Kabeljauwse factions in Holland.

Like other minor states, Gelderland often waged war on its neighbours. The most powerful of these was the duchy of Brabant.

The duchy of Brabant

Brabant, with its fertile lands and with the wealth brought by the trade of its towns along the Meuse and Scheldt rivers, had developed into a major power, influencing politics all over North West Europe. Thus, the Dukes of Brabant were important figures in the German Empire, for example intervening in the struggle between the Staufen and the Welfen, the two family-parties that contested each other the imperial crown (1198-1214); cleverly, playing the one against the other they succeeded in enlarging their own power. However, this policy brought them into conflict with England and France, which also supported either the Welfian or the Staufian candidates for the throne.

During the mid-thirteenth century, the Brabant dukes got involved in the county of Holland. In 1248, Henry II of Brabant supported the election of William II, Count of Holland, as King of the Romans, which would eventually bring him the imperial crown. However, William, who was ambitious, tried to use his new position to gain possession of prosperous Flanders, which resulted in a struggle with Brabant. He was prevented from accomplishing his plans, and gaining the imperial crown, when he was killed during a campaign against the West-Frisians in 1256.

Brabant had its golden age between 1267 and 1355. Prospects had not been

Funerary monument of Gerard IV, Count of Guelders, and his wife Margaretha of Brabant, in the minster of Roermond, ca 1230. It is the oldest sepulchral monument in the Netherlands and the oldest showing a married couple in medieval Europe

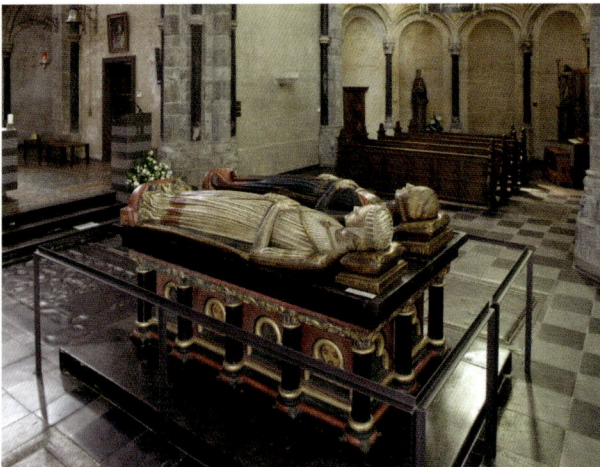

favourable when Henry III died in 1261. A disruptive struggle for the succession, like those in other principalities, seemed inevitable. Henry's eldest son and heir, another Henry, was mentally and physically handicapped. Henry's widow succeeded in becoming her son's regent, but had to permit co-guardianship to her most influential neighbours, Count Otto II of Gelderland and the Prince-Bishop of Liège. This arrangement, made with the support of the clergy, the aristocracy and the towns, gathered in the so-called 'States' of Brabant, averted a dynastic crisis and assured peace.

When Henry IV came of age he renounced his rights at an assembly of the States, after which he entered a monastery. His younger brother John succeeded him to become one of the most colourful dukes in the history of the duchy.

The 'joyous entry'

When In 1355, Duke John III died without male issue, he was succeeded by his daughter Joanna. On this occasion a charter was drawn up to specify the rights of the towns as opposed to those of the ducal government. Obviously, as this act favoured the interests of trade and industry, concentrated in urban centres, the occasion indicated the growing importance of urban economic power for state government since tax-income came increasingly to rely on urban riches. Gone were the times wherein the great landed estates, owned by the aristocracy, had been the only sources of wealth; gone, also, the times wherein the nobles had been the main and often only power in the land.

The 1355-act was called the 'Joyous Entry' as it was confirmed by the new duchess's solemn entry into the Brabant towns that now offered their loyalty. It literally sealed a political development in which Brabant actually preceded other regions, by defining the relations between the sovereign and his subjects in a written, wax-sealed document stating the rights and duties of both parties. For fourteenth-century Brabant it was an occasion of the greatest moment: a contract between the prince and his people. Specifically, the 'Joyous Entry' was a guarantee to the towns that the duke would not start a costly war without their permission. It also enabled them to make sure that tax revenues, largely originating in the towns, were spent wisely.

Friesland

Unlike the states described above, Friesland never had a ruling family of its own. A series of lords from the House of Bruno, from Brunswick, were in power there during the eleventh century. Little is known about them, but their coins, struck in various Frisian towns, have been found as far away as Russia, indicating the continued importance of Frisian trade.

Actually, Frisia consisted of several small counties such as Staveren - which had been granted to the bishophric of Utrecht in 1077 - and Oost-

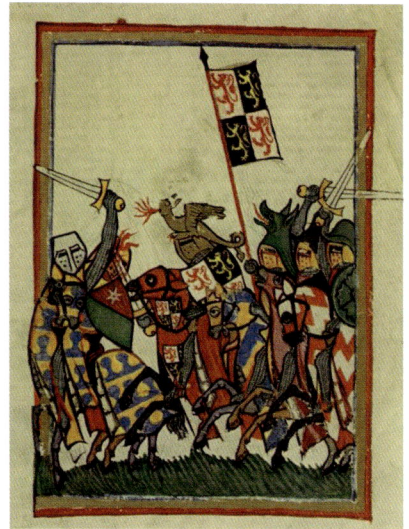

Duke Jan I of Brabant battling at Woeringen (1288) for the possession of the duchy of Limburg

The marriage in 1418 of Jan IV, Duke of Brabant, with the reigning Countess of Holland, Zeeland and Hainault, Jacqueline of Bavaria

ergo and Westergo, roughly corresponding respectively to the east and west of Friesland as it is today.

When Egbert II, the last of the Bruno's, rebelled against his liege lord, the German Emperor Henry IV, in 1089 Oostergo and Westergo were taken away from him and also granted as a fief to the Bishop of Utrecht, much to the chagrin of Holland that coveted these lands for itself and certainly did not like to see the power of its major neighbour thus enlarged.

Consequently, during the twelfth century the bishops of Utrecht and the counts of Holland began to dispute each other the possession of the Frisian counties; these, however, were not inclined to obey either ruler. Emperor Frederick Barbarossa eventually decided to allow Utrecht and Holland joint government over Friesland.

In 1197, William, the brother of the ruling count of Holland, was appointed count of Friesland but he had little time to establish his authority. In 1203, on the death of his brother, he also became count of Holland. In the absence of their lord, the Frisians no longer felt accountable to him. They were free once more. Feuds now broke out between several of the great landowning families who attacked each other from their strongholds with small armies. This strife, comparable, again, to that in other principalities, was aggravated by the influence of the mighty monasteries of the Cistercian and Norbertine religious Orders. The majority of monks in Frisian monasteries during the thirteenth century were lay brothers who had not taken the major vows. Amongst them, monastic discipline slackened or even disappeared altogether. In about 1340, a feud broke out between the great monasteries of Bloemkamp and Lidlum. Bloemkamp was a Cistercian foundation. After their habits, the monks belonging to this Order were called grey, or 'schiere', friars, or 'Schieringers'. This also accounts for the name of the island Schiermonnikoog which belonged to the monastery at that time. The monks of Lidlum were part of the Norbertine Order. Because their wealth was

mainly based on cattle, they were known as 'Vetkopers' (butter sellers). Therefore Frisian party-feuds were described as the struggle between the 'Schieringers' and the 'Vetkopers'.

This struggle flared up continually during the second half of the fourteenth and the entire fifteenth century, when peasants and burghers, clergy and laymen and the various noble families all fought among themselves and against each other. The Schieringers, who dominated in Oostergo were usually in favour of Frisian independence. The Vetkopers, who lived mainly in what is now the Province of Friesland, were inclined to join forces with Holland. These feuds led to plundering, raiding and arson, causing great harm to the Frisian people who lacked a higher authority to protect them.

Occasionally one of the counts of Holland attempted to claim the rights of Holland over Friesland, still formally valid. In 1345, William IV raised a large army in order to subdue the Frisians. However, he was killed and his army soundly defeated during the Battle of Warns, a village in the southwest of Friesland.

At the end of the fourteenth century, renewed attempts to re-establish the authority of the Holland counts over Friesland also met with failure. However, the Frisians did lose their freedom after all, at the end of the fifteenth century. Yet, they did not lose it to the counts of Holland but to a descendant of the Burgundian dukes, who had now become Holy Roman Emperor. Charles V subjected rebellious Friesland, appointing a 'stadhouder' or lieutenant to govern this unruly people in his name.

Memorial tablet of the viscount of Montfoort, ca 1380. It is said to be the oldest portrait painting of the Netherlands

8   Economy and politics since c. 1000: the beginnings of an urban economy

Construction of dykes and reclamation of land

After the turn of the millennium, with the Vikings ceasing their raids, the climate getting milder and, consequently, conditions for regular agrarian production improving, the population began to increase. Also, the political situation stabilized, creating peace and order. To meet the need for more land by the people who still lived mainly by farming and cattle breeding, wasteland now was increasingly cultivated. Also, low-lying areas were drained and protected by dykes, and marshland was reclaimed. The farmers of Holland and Friesland became so skilled at this work that, in 1113, the Archbishop of Hamburg offered them land in Saxony for reclamation. In this way they helped to colonize and populate eastern Germany.

In addition to the need for more land, the rising sea level, caused by the gradual melting of the polar ice, also necessitated the construction of dykes. Well into the thirteenth century seawater poured into the Netherlands via the Almere. The construction of sea dykes, such as the dyke between Harlingen and Stavoren, in Friesland, became a dire necessity to save the country from regular inundation and siltation.

Organizations called 'water boards' were now formed to ensure the dykes were kept in good repair and to regulate the water level in low-lying areas. This was one example of a general tendency to order and regulate everyday life.

The same tendency was also noticeable in the Church, where a re-organization of the dioceses took place involving the appointment of archdeacons and suffragan bishops. At a lower level, large parishes were split up into a number of smaller ones, with boundaries corresponding roughly to those of a village; all this helped to increase the authorities' hold on religious life and the community.

However, with the population growing, the need for fuel increased, which resulted in large-scale peat cutting. This created sometimes huge lakes that, in themselves, threatened the people's safety. Soon, the authorities had to order people to plant trees in their farmyards and along the roads, to remedy this problem.

The economy and the monasteries

The first monasteries in the Netherlands often were established by the rich and the powerful: the regional princes and the nobles. For instance, Rijnsburg Abbey was founded by Countess Petronella of Holland in 1133.

Many monasteries became huge establishments, housing large communities of, sometimes, as many as a thousand inmates. Most monasteries were situated in the countryside, not only because as yet there were few large towns but also because, having to support themselves, their main activity besides their spiritual life was the management of their often ex-

The romantic ruins of the once-famous abbey of Rijnsburg, probably painted by Albert Cuyp between 1640 and 1642

tensive estates; over time, they became an important force in shaping both nature and culture, for the monks were foremost in constructing dykes and pioneers in reclaiming land and cultivating wasteland, thus improving agricultural production, increasing prosperity and generally contributing to the welfare of society at large.

In the fourteenth century, smaller monasteries arose, usually with a more contemplative background. They were not situated in the rural areas, but in the towns that had been founded during the preceding centuries. By now, a growing urban population felt the need for spiritual care, but also for the kind of education that only the literate monks and nuns were able to provide.

The growing importance of towns

The resurgence of old towns, dating from the Roman period, as well as, after the crisis of the ninth and tenth centuries, the rise of new towns during the eleventh and twelfth centuries, was partly due to population growth. However, it also was influenced by the slow but steady increase in trade and industry. The food situation improved with higher production through higher yield ratios and better transport of grain and other food-stuffs. While towns basically thrived on trade and manufacture, they drew produce from the surrounding rural areas at the weekly markets and annu-al fairs. Supplies of wood and other primary provisions had to be brought in for the daily needs of the townspeople who increasingly did not produce these themselves. For people now could afford to specialize, both in agri-culture and in industry, and make a better profit by producing for the in-terregional market. The increase in trade resulted in growing commercial prosperity that, in its turn, induced investment in the arts.

During the eleventh and twelfth centuries, Europe renewed and stepped up its commercial contacts with important overseas regions. Trade with the Near East, rich in luxury goods from all over farther Asia, was resumed after the first crusade in 1096. England, which was able to produce huge quantities of wool for the textile industry, was enmeshed in a continental trade network after William, duke of Normandy, had conquered it in 1066. Soon, the towns in the Netherlands found themselves on a crossroads of continental trade routes, a position that was to prove very advantageous.

New trade routes

As trade increased, and the range of products grew in number and volume, larger ships were needed which, however, could not navigate the old inland waterways. Other trade routes now came into use, including one over the North Sea through the Danish Sound into the Baltic Sea. This meant that new markets came within reach, such as the rich Baltic ports, where there was a plentiful supply of grain and wood for shipping to the Netherlands; there, merchants saw a possibility to export such goods to southern markets, returning with products that could be profitably sold in the north.

Soon, such old trading centres as Tiel and Utrecht, which depended on the great rivers to transport their merchandise, could no longer compete with the seaports in the north such as Stavoren, Leeuwarden, Groningen, Dokkum and Bolsward. From these ports merchant ships set out for the German states, England and the Scottish kingdom.

The Hansa towns

Merchants from towns on the Zuiderzee and the IJssel-river, including Harderwijk, Elburg, Deventer and Kampen, also navigated the Danish Sound; this was known as 'around-country shipping', or 'Ommelandvaart'. Many of these towns joined the Hanseatic League, probably the first truly international trade organization, ever: a merchant guild uniting numerous German and Dutch trading towns to defend their joint interests.

The independent position taken by these towns in economic affairs was partly due to the increased freedom of town councils to decide their own fate rather than having to obey princely orders. Such freedom was increasingly incorporated in the town charter, confirmed by the ruler of the region to which the town belonged. In return for granting towns such privileges, the princes hoped to gain financial support in their wars from the ever richer and more powerful merchants. One of the earliest examples of a charter of this kind dates from 1185, in which Duke Henry I of Brabant confirmed the privileges of 's Hertogenbosch. Later charters

in the Dutch regions often followed the pattern set in this document. Thus, the privileges granted to Haarlem and 's Gravenzande in 1245 by Count William II of Holland were based on those of "Den Bosch".

Seal of Duke Jan II of Brabant (1275–1312)
Stadsarchief
's Hertogenbosch

17**th**-century painting
showing the Weighing
House of Deventer
photo: Binnendijk
Deventer

The growing political power of the towns

The wealth and the relative political and institutional independence afforded by their privileges enabled towns to become political players alongside the other power groups: the ruler and his bureaucracy, the aristocracy and the Church. By the fifteenth century, many towns operated almost independently. Inevitably, they also became a strong and sometimes decisive political force in the many party feuds dividing the various states. They often intervened in princely successions, knowing from experience how damaging the resulting wars could be: they cost money and hampered trade.

No longer did town councils unquestioningly submit to taxation or the obligation to take part in a war. Like the aristocracy, they first wanted to

Fictional portrait of
Count William V of
Holland (1349-1358)

be consulted by the central government. In most principalities, this led to the increasingly regular convening of consultative meetings between representatives of the three 'estates', i.e. the clergy, the aristocracy and the towns.

The first of these more or less regular assemblies was convened in Brabant, in 1312, when Duke John II, forced to ensure the co-operation of his mighty subjects, issued the so-called Charter of Kortenberg, calling for a council of fourteen members to be formed, comprising four members of the aristocracy, and ten representatives of the towns. As stated above, the right of this council to be consulted on certain matters of state later was confirmed in the 'joyous entry'.

In 1362, during the rule of Count William V, the joint Estates of the counties of Holland, Zeeland and Hainault drew up new regulations to give themselves comparable political influence. In The Sticht, the burghers of the city of Utrecht already had acquired a say in the election of a new bishop in the twelfth century. Finally, the Utrecht Estates' right to assemble was confirmed in the 'Charter for the Land' issued in 1375 by Bishop Arnold of Horn, who had been obliged to make concessions after the unfortunate outcome of a war against Holland and Gelderland.

In Gelre, too, fear over a troubled and troublesome succession prompted the aristocracy and the towns to join forces and convince the duke he had better seek the co-operation of the political-economic elite of his duchy before taking major decisions. Duke Reynold IV acknowledged the rights of the 'States of Gelderland' in 1419. Thus, by the fourteenth century, in most early Dutch states, some form of consensual government, however oligarchic, was growing.

The original text of the
so-called 'Charter of
Kortenberg' (1312), that
gave some influence
in ducal policy to the
representatives of the
Brabant nobility and
towns
Stadsarchief
's Hertogenbosch

9   Culture: the role of the urban bourgeoisie

The rise of the towns had other effects besides economic and political ones. Till the eleventh century, cultural activity in the fields of the arts and sciences mainly was confined to the aristocracy and the clergy. Particularly in the monasteries, Greek and Latin texts were preserved and copied. Moreover, by the thirteenth century, the first chronicles recording contemporary life were written, by such monks as Emo and Menko. Both, incidentally, later became abbot of the Bloemkamp monastery in Groningen.

In monastic culture, Latin was the language used for writing. But both at the princely courts and, as a result of the rising importance of towns,

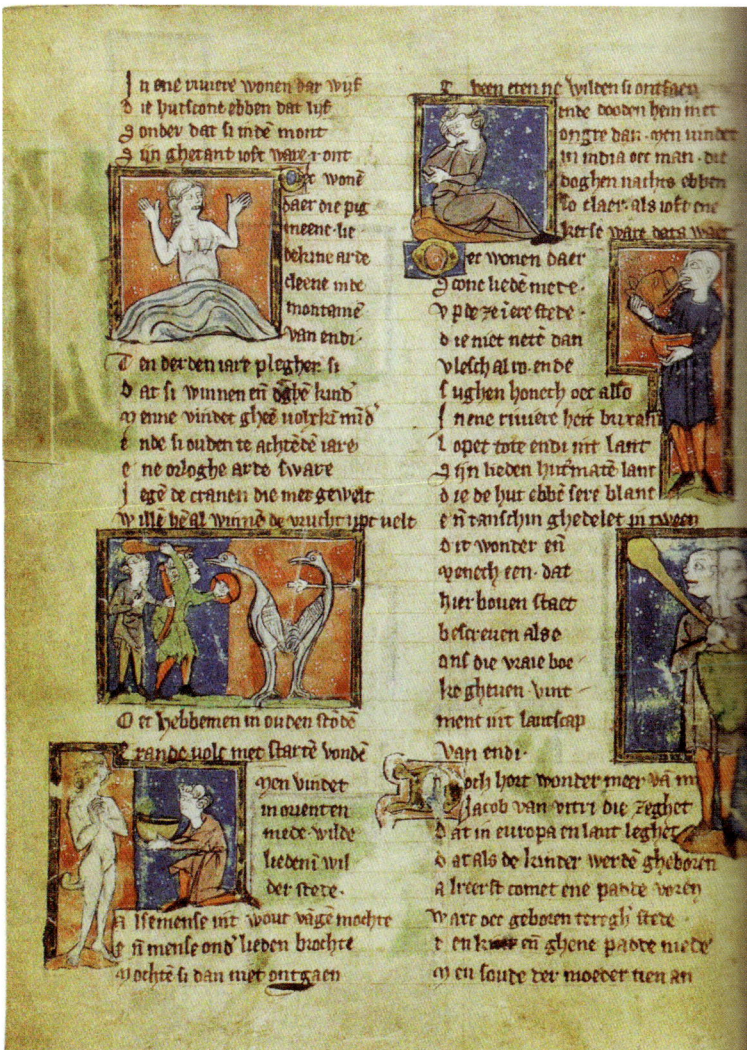

Illustrated page from Jacob van Maerlant's famous 'encyclopedia' on nature, written 1270

The minster at Roermond, one of the grandest late-Romanesque churches of the Netherlands. Building started in the early 13th century

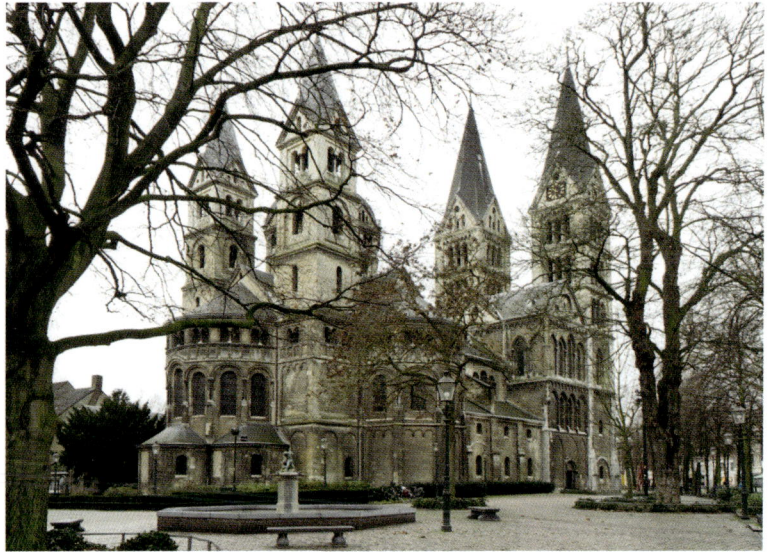

amongst the burgher elite, a form of Dutch vernacular was used increasingly to record the urban experience of life. The 'Verse Chronicle' of Melis Stoke, dating from soon after 1300, and the works of Jacob van Maerlant are good examples of a new, urban culture. Though religion continued to permeate every aspect of life, in these less markedly Church-dominated surroundings a more secular view of man and the world developed as well.

As far as these times have left any architectural remains at all, they tend to be specimens of ecclesiastical architecture.

The Romanesque style, particularly in the north, was mainly the art of the rural regions: buildings typically had massive walls, the small windows and the doors were spanned with rounded arches, and the towers were simple saddle-roofed structures. Many fine examples of this sturdy and yet elegant way of building survive in the villages of the northern provinces of Groningen and Friesland.

Romanesque architecture in the south of the country, represented by the lovely churches of St. Servatius and of Our Lady in Maastricht, is more monumental and represents another fashion, known as the Maasland-style. Famed, too, for its wrought-iron work, this style reached its peak in the eleventh and twelfth centuries. It produced magnificent reliquaries, the most splendid of which is, arguably, the shrine of St. Servatius, still kept in the church devoted to him.

Of course, there were craftsmen working in iron, silver and gold in the North, too, but they did not achieve the high standard of the South. What is left of their work consists mainly of coins and monastic seals, including that of Egmond Abbey. The oldest surviving shrine from the North was made in Utrecht in 1362.

During the fourteenth and fifteenth centuries a lighter and more elegant architecture, later called Gothic, developed in the towns. It created ever more complex churches, their walls pierced by stained-glass windows and dissolving in pinnacles and turrets, the whole crowned with huge spires.

The most famous fourteenth-century Gothic buildings in this country can be seen in Utrecht and 's Hertogenbosch. Constructing the tower of the Dom-church in Utrecht began in 1321, against the criticism of those who condemned it as both arrogant and wasteful. It was designed by a master builder, who, unlike most of his colleagues during these ages, is known by name: Jan van Henegouwen, or Hainault, a county in the far South where new artistic styles had arrived from northern France. It was completed in 1382. The choir also dates from the fourteenth century. With the tower, some 110 meters high, it is all that remains of this once great cathedral, as the grand nave was destroyed. The perhaps even more magnificent cathedral of St. John in the town of 's Hertogenbosch was built in the same period.

The best-known example of a secular Gothic building is the 'Ridderzaal' or Knights' Hall in The Hague, built at the end of the thirteenth century for Count Floris V of Holland. This hall, which has been restored in the 19th century to conform to the then ideas of what a medieval building should have looked like, is the scene of the annual ceremony of the opening of Parliament by the Dutch sovereign.

The fine arts

Large-scale painting does not seem to have really flourished in the Netherlands until the fourteenth century. On the other hand, various artists developed a high skill in miniature painting, usually to illustrate the manuscripts written in the monasteries. Obviously, this art form was but little influenced by the awakening cultural activity of the towns. Its few surviving examples are to be found in missals made for nobles and high-placed clergymen, particularly in Utrecht and Gelderland.

While before 1350 monumental painting was rare, in the following decades churches were decorated with elaborate murals, of which, however, few survive. Indeed, there may have existed quite a lot of these frescoes, but probably most were destroyed during the iconoclast fury of the late-sixteenth century Reformation. Also dating to the late fourteenth century are a few painted panels, most of which were made in Gelderland and Utrecht, too. Finally, there were the memorial tableaux, placed in churches near the tombs of high-ranking persons.

Sculpture from this period is rare as well. The few remaining works are mainly monuments to nobles and high-ranking clergy, such as the tomb of Jan van Arkel in the great church at Gorinchem, or Gorcum.

Reliquary of St. Servatius. One of the finest examples of 12th-century silversmith's work in the 'Maasland–Romanesque' style

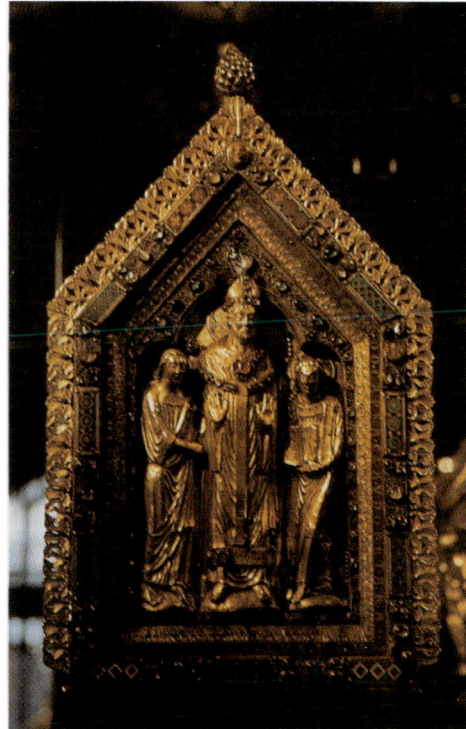

In the fifteenth century, with wealth increasing in Holland, Zeeland and Utrecht through profits made both in agriculture and in trade and industry, the affluent citizens became interested in showing their material and also political power, as well as in adorning their homes and towns. Portraits were now widely produced - documenting the continuity of patrician families, and showing the visitor an impressive public 'face' - but landscapes, too, became increasingly popular. Meanwhile, small devotional paintings testify to the continued importance of religion.

Religion in the towns

In general, all culture in this period silently but evocatively reflects the essential part played by religion in everyday life. Until the fourteenth century, the aristocracy and the clergy still were the leading patrons of the arts. By now, however, the class of wealthy burghers that had developed in the towns was gradually gaining prominence. Significantly, in religion too, this new class showed itself susceptible to new trends.

The establishment of small monasteries in the towns, besides the big ones that continued to flourish in the countryside, was mentioned above. Many of these new foundations were rooted in the Modern Devotion, a movement started by Geert Grote of Deventer c. 1384. Its object was to induce as broad as possible a range of lay people to return to a simpler way of life based on the basic values of Christianity. Perhaps surprisingly, these ideas predominantly appealed to well-educated and wealthy citizens. They now formed and joined religious brotherhoods or congregations, without taking vows, however. Soon, these groups associated themselves with existing monastic Orders, usually the Franciscans, famous for their poverty and piety.

Meanwhile, education was the main instrument of the Modern Devotion. To be effective, however, it had to reach out to other than elite children, only, and did indeed try to do so. This resulted in an increase of the number of town schools, in an increased production of religious tracts, mostly of a moral nature, and, perhaps, also in increased literacy.

Book of Hours said to have belonged to the Humanist Geert Grote (1340-1384)

10 Society and politics in the Burgundian–Habsburg Empire: centralization of power and authority 1350–1550

During the period from the tenth to the fourteenth century, a number of regional states had been formed in the region, now often called the Low Countries. At a much later stage, i.e. in the early nineteenth century, they transformed into the provinces of the present kingdoms of the Netherlands and of Belgium.

Arguably, an important part of the character of the Netherlands was formed during this time, both in its geographic and economic, and its political and cultural aspects. Specifically, towards the end of this period, the towns started taking their place in the political arena besides the traditional rulers: the sovereign princes, the aristocracy and the clergy. At the same time, society in the Netherlands gradually became more urban and the culture of the affluent burghers set the tone.

The situation from c. 1350 onwards

Around c. 1350, most of the future provinces of the Netherlands already had been established as independent states that only nominally accepted the suzerainty of the Holy Roman Emperor. Yet, by the same time, the authority of the various regional dynasties was dwindling, due to internal conflicts and the growing power of the urban burgher elite. In most states, the assemblies of nobles, clergy and burghers imposed all kinds of limits on the rulers, mainly aimed at curbing expenditure and, hence, taxation.

During the fifteenth century, two contrasting developments occurred. On the one hand many towns evolved into small but powerful little states, going their own way. On the other hand the power over the various principalities slowly was concentrated in the hands of one single family, that of the Dukes of Burgundy, who acquired it through judicious marriages and the subsequent inheritances, and through outright wars.

Philip the Bold (1342–1404) and his matrimonial policy

In 1363, the then king of France gave the French Duchy of Burgundy to his son Philip, surnamed the Bold, who married Margaretha of Flanders, in her own right heiress to the independent County of Burgundy (Franche-Comté) in 1369. In 1384, on the death of his father in law, Philip, through his wife, now also inherited the states of Flanders, Artois, Nevers and Rethel, as well as two important towns that had been conquered from Brabant: Antwerp and Mechlin.

From then on, the Burgundian dukes operated largely independently from, and mostly in opposition to the kings of France. Although in the ensuing struggles they lost some ground on their southern borders, they successfully continued to extend their power northwards.

Philip succeeded in arranging favourable marriages for his children. In 1385, a double wedding took place, the one between his son John, later

Duke Philip the Bold of Burgundy

known as John the Fearless, and Margaretha of Bavaria, and the other between his daughter Margaretha and the brother of Margaretha of Bavaria, William VI, who became Count of Holland, Zeeland and Hainault in 1404. As the latter had no son, on his death in 1417 he was succeeded by his daughter Jacqueline of Bavaria who at that time was married to Duke

John IV of Brabant. Inevitably, problems brewed between Burgundy with its Flemish states and the Holland-Brabant conglomerate.

Philip the Good (1396-1467)

Philip, surnamed the Good, son of John the Fearless, succeeded in uniting all these regions under his rule. He soon engaged in a fierce struggle with his cousin Jacqueline, who, despite her successive marriages, had born no children to succeed her in her own dignities. During these feuds, the disputes between the factions of the Hoeksen and the Kabeljauwsen flared up again, with the one siding with the countess and the other supporting the claims of the duke. Soon, the groups were fighting as bitterly as ever. Finally, in 1428, a compromise was reached. This entailed that Jacqueline relinquished her real power to Philip, while keeping her titles. Neither was she free to remarry without the permission of Philip, of her mother, who played a rather devious role, and of the assemblies of her three states. When, in spite of this treaty, she secretly married the Zeeland noble Frank van Borselen, she forfeited her titles and Philip succeeded her as Count of Holland, Zeeland and Hainault.

Brabant had already come into Philip's possession in 1430 because his two ducal cousins had died childless. In 1451, he also inherited Luxembourg with the result that, in addition to the ancestral part of Burgundy, his 'empire' then included the present territory of Belgium, Luxembourg and a large chunk of the Netherlands. Gelderland, Utrecht, Friesland and Groningen were not part of it, yet. Still, in 1456 Utrecht, and with it Overijssel and Drenthe were brought into the Burgundian camp when Philip succeeded in having his bastard son David appointed bishop, there.

Friesland stayed out of Burgundian reach for a long time. Groningen too, held on to its independence for the time being, with occasional support from the Dukes of Gelderland who came to look upon the encroaching Burgundians as their archenemies, and, consequently, became the toughest opponents of Burgundian expansion.

Charles the Bold (1433-1477)

Like his father before him, Charles the Bold, Philip's son and heir, came into conflict with Gelderland. He had high hopes for his growing collection of states, seeking to expand it to equal the size of the ninth century Carolingian state of the Emperor Lothair. Moreover, he hoped to seal his triumphal conquests by gaining the title of king from the Holy Roman Emperor.

Forced to deftly manoeuvre in international politics, Charles formed an alliance with the English against the French. The English king, himself an

Duke Philip the Good of Burgundy, also Count of Holland, Zeeland and Hainault, and, by inheritance, duke of Brabant and Luxemburg. Copy after the original by Rogier van der Weyden

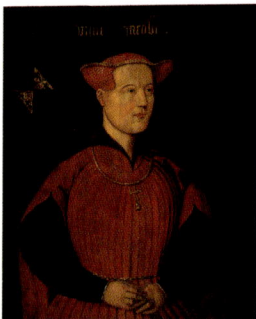

Jacqueline of Bavaria (1401-1436), Countess of Holland, Zeeland and Hainault

Meeting of the knights of the Order of the Golden Fleece, founded by Duke Philip the Good of Burgundy (1430)

enemy of France that during the Hundred Years' War had recaptured most of the territories formerly held by the English, was willing to support the Burgundians in their struggle, which grew more bitter as Burgundy grew more powerful. In another move, Charles annexed Gelderland to the Burgundian conglomerate in 1473. He conquered Lorraine in the same year, thus making sure that his many states in the Netherlands now adjoined his original Burgundian lands. However, in 1476 the people of Lorraine rebelled. In 1477, the duke was killed in an attempt to regain the capital, Nancy. He was succeeded by his only child, his daughter Mary, who had been promised in marriage to the Emperor's son. When she did marry this Maximilian of Habsburg, Archduke of Austria, of the family which had pro-

Duke Charles the Bold of Burgundy (1433 – 1477)

Map of the Burgundian
Netherlands at the
death of Charles the
Bold (1433–1477)

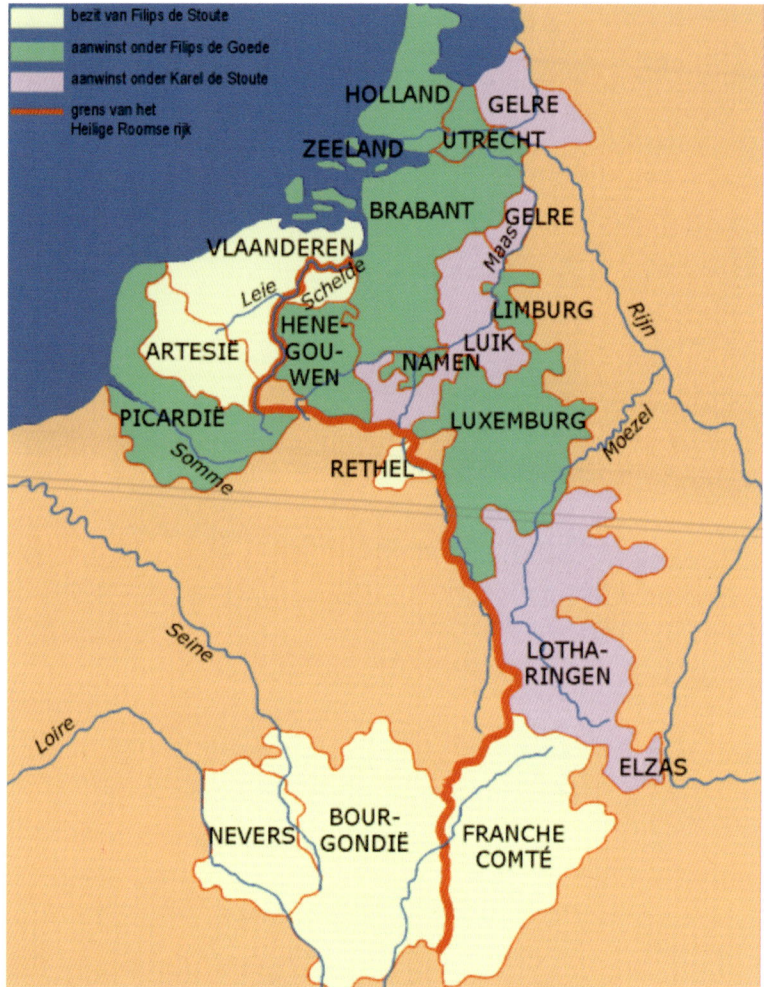

bezit van Filips de Stoute
aanwinst onder Filips de Goede
aanwinst onder Karel de Stoute
grens van het
Heilige Roomse rijk

HOLLAND
GELRE
ZEELAND
UTRECHT
BRABANT
GELRE
VLAANDEREN
Leie
Schelde
Maas
LIMBURG
Rijn
HENE-
GOU-
WEN
ARTESIE
LUIK
NAMEN
PICARDIE
LUXEMBURG
Moezel
Somme
RETHEL
Seine
LOTHA-
RINGEN
Loire
ELZAS
NEVERS
BOUR-
GONDIE
FRANCHE
COMTÉ

Duchess Mary of
Burgundy (1457–1482)

duced German emperors for many decades, the Burgundian states and the Habsburg family lands were united.

Meanwhile, the Hoeksen-faction in Holland continued to oppose the dukes of Burgundy, attempting to undermine their authority as best it could. However, the rebels were driven over the border to the city of Utrech from where, between 1481 and 1483, they carried on a violent struggle against Bishop David of Burgundy and Maximilian of Habsburg, by now Holy Roman Emperor as well as, through his wife Mary of Burgundy, in her lieu the acting new count of Holland. Mary died in 1482, and Maximilian was appointed regent for their son and heir Philip, later known as Philip the Fair. The Hoeksen had to admit defeat at Utrecht in 1483. However, in 1488 they returned to the field against the Burgundians and even succeeded in taking the city of Rotterdam, only to be defeated again two years later.

Meanwhile Gelderland was more successful in freeing itself from Burgundian bondage. Philip the Fair, who came of age in 1493, at first did not cherish the idea of subjecting Gelderland once more. But since his father Maximilian insisted on it, he conquered the duchy in 1504. Charles, Duke of Gelderland, then formed an alliance with the French king who greatly feared his Burgundian cousins. He attempted to regain his lands by means of raids headed by the dreaded military commander Maarten van Rossum. With the help of, among others, the Frisian pirate "Grote Pier", for a time he also succeeded in subduing Groningen and Friesland. Groningen then acknowledged him as its overlord.

Burgundy, Habsburg and the world: Philip the Fair (1478–1506)

Archduke Maximilian of Habsburg-Austria (1459–1519)

Surveying the titles of Philip the Fair, it will be clear how mighty Burgundy had become. He not only was Duke of Burgundy, he also was count or duke of more than a dozen of the Low Countries. As his father's son he also was Archduke of Austria. His power increased even more when, in 1495, he married Joanna of Castile, the only remaining heir to her mother's kingdom of Castile and her father's kingdom of Aragon. These two states subsequently became the heart of Spain as it is today. In 1506, on the death of his mother in law, Philip became King of Castile, and, with it, of Castile's recently acquired American possessions. However, in the same year he unexpectedly died.

Duke Philip the Fair of Burgundy (1478–1506) and his wife Princess Joanna of Aragon and Castile (1479–1555)

The Netherlands as part of a global empire: Emperor Charles V (1500–1558)

Because of the marriage of Philip the Fair and Joanna of Castile and Aragon, their eldest son Charles was destined to inherit an empire that already was beginning to span the world. Yet, his roots lay in the Netherlands, as he had been born in Ghent, in 1500, and had been educated in the Humanist tradition by the scholar Adriaen Boeyens, who hailed from Utrecht. Through Charles's influence, Adriaen later was made a cardinal and, eventually, was chosen pope. Thus, Hadrian VI became the first Dutch successor of St. Peter. He was not much loved in Rome because of his stern policy against the Church's mismanagement and decadence. Maybe for that reason, he was the last non-Italian pope till the end of the twentieth century.

On the death of his father in 1506, Charles came into the entire Burgundian inheritance, including the many still independent duchies and counties that, together, were now being called 'the Netherlands'. He was declared of age in 1515, and in 1516, on the death of his grandfather Ferdinand who had governed Castile as regent since 1506, he also became king of both the Spanish kingdoms, Aragon - with its subsidiary kingdom of Naples-Sicily and the Duchy of Milan -, and Castile, which also included the kingdom of Granada, conquered in 1492, and the Castilian claims on the New World established after Columbus's voyages in 1492: Mexico, which was conquered in 1519 by Spanish adventurers; Peru, taken from the Inca's in 1532, and the Philippine islands, acquired in the same decades. Charles also inherited the Austrian States on the death of his grandfather Maximilian in 1519. Finally, by dint of much intrigue and bribery he was elected King of the Romans and duly crowned Emperor of the Holy Roman Empire.

Meanwhile, though the duchy of Burgundy itself had been reconquered by France, Gelderland, Groningen, Friesland and Utrecht had been added to the Burgundian empire. In 1543, Gelderland at last surrendered to Charles V, accepting the Treaty of Venlo. Groningen had already acknowledged him as overlord in 1536, and in the Sticht, too, he had acquired the secular power of the bishop through the decision of his former tutor, now Pope Hadrian. Yet, all the regions of this vast empire remained independent administrative entities.

Having succeeded in uniting the 'Seventeen Netherlands' as one contiguous territory, Charles did not wish to rule them as separate states. Accepting that he could not rule in person, given his obligations elsewhere, he appointed a royal governor-general, to be stationed in Brussels. Preferring trustworthy relations to fill this hugely important position, since Charles knew that much of his wealth came from these unruly regions, he first chose his formidable aunt Margaretha, dowager-duchess of Savoy. Later, she was succeeded by his sister Mary, dowager-queen of Hungary.

From that time onwards, he himself only occasionally visited the Netherlands, spending most of his time fighting his enemies: France, which, understandably, opposed the Habsburgs who now were encircling it; the

Titian's famous portrait of Emperor Charles V (1548)

princes of the German Empire, who resented an emperor who tried to rule rather than reign, only, and the new phenomenon of the religious rebels, the Protestants of the German states. Last, but not least, he had to combat the armies of the Islamic Turks, advancing on his empire both on the Balkans and across the Mediterranean.

The Parliament of
Mechlin/Malines (1474),
the high court of the
Burgundian–Habsburg
states

The seventeen Netherlands and their cities
oppose the Habsburg policy of centralization

From the late fifteenth century onwards, the regional representative assemblies, the 'Estates', composed of representatives of the clergy, the aristocracy and the towns, developed into the strongest opponents of the central authority which the Burgundians and Habsburgs were trying to establish. Formally, the Burgundian Habsburgs ruled each of these regions separately: as duke, count or lord. However, they felt that a common policy and administration for all the Netherlands was necessary, if only to improve their tax income from these states' fiscal resources, which of course they needed to pay for the wars they waged to safeguard their

enormous empire. To them, scrupulously respecting regional privileges and maintaining the sovereignty of each state was less than efficient, administratively as well as politically. Therefore, they proceeded to set up a well-oiled civil service headed by a chancellor in each and every state. In addition, they appointed an advisory body, a council of high-ranking nobles, professional administrators and lawyers. Also, they established chambers of accounts and courts of justice. However, finding procedures cumbersome and not easy to control, they soon centralized fiscal and judicial administration: a central General Chamber of Accounts already had been created by Charles the Bold, and soon a Supreme Court known as the Parliament of Mechlin/Malines was instituted as well.

To counteract the Burgundian efforts towards fiscal and legal centralization, a number of towns supported those groups who turned against the power of the dukes. Thus, Utrecht and Amersfoort took sides in the battles between the Hoeksen and Kabeljauwsen between 1481 and 1483.

Also, both cities denied the Episcopal judge power of jurisdiction in case of capital crimes committed within their walls. Soon, they decided to elect their own town council as well, which then drew up city statutes and even went so far as to appoint the bailiff, traditionally the local representative of princely power. Inexorably, however, in the sixteenth century, central Burgundian-Habsburg government in the various states managed to curb the independence of the cities, though the burghers continued to influence princely government through their participation in the regional assemblies.

The States-General and the Grand Council

However, the various regional assemblies, too, were affected by centralization. In 1464, for the first time they convened together, at Bruges, to decide whether Duke Philip the Good should be financially enabled to go on a crusade. The meeting was called the "States-General" and soon became a permanent feature in the government of the Burgundian lands, the more so since they succeeded in having their role inscribed in the "Grand Privilege" issued by Mary of Burgundy in 1477, when on the death of her father she wanted her Habsburg husband acknowledged as ruler of all her states. The States-General demanded that from now on they would be allowed to meet if it pleased them, rather than on the monarch's order, only, and that the ruler would never start a war without their consent. Also, the Parliament of Mechlin and the General Chamber of Accounts, the most hated instruments of central authority, were abolished and a Grand Council was formed with 25 members and a chancellor to assist the duchess in her government.

Anonymous Dutch portrait c. 1550 of Mary of Hungary (1505–1558), royal governor-general of the Netherlands 1531–1555
RMA

The Burgundian-Habsburg rulers did not fail to retaliate. In 1504, the Parliament of Mechlin was reinstated as a Supreme Court, though the States-General managed to retain their powers. Charles V, trying to make the Grand Council into a centralizing instrument of his own, set it up as a Council of Finances, a Privy Council and a Council of State. Whereas the first two were completely dominated by him, the last, meant to be a general advisory council, consisted of leading civil servants and the major nobles of the Netherlands, whose sometimes independent stance he feared. But effectively the Emperor's governors who ruled in Brussels mostly consulted with the civil servants, their preferred instruments of central power.

The economy: the growing importance of the towns of Holland

After c. 1350, the population of Europe had declined dramatically due to a small 'ice age'; as average temperature on earth dropped, if only to a small degree, agriculture suffered; a series of failed harvests led to famine and endemic physical weakness, and hundreds of thousands of people fell prey to devastating epidemics, such as the Great Plaque. The resulting economic depression lasted well into the fifteenth century, when the first signs of recovery showed. Grain now was needed in the whole of Western Europe, because the population expanded again. Most countries could not produce enough, but the Baltic region and Central Europe offered a rich supply.

Precisely through its traditional trading connections, Holland was now beginning to dominate the economy of the Netherlands. Since the fourteenth century, Dordrecht already had been playing a leading part, trading

The Drapers' Hall at Leiden, built in 1640

between the North Sea region and Central Europe via the great rivers. In 1344, the town even acquired the staple right for all traffic on the Rhine.

After c. 1400, other Holland towns began to join in international trade, especially to the Baltic. The major organization to suffer was the great late-medieval trade-network of the Hansa. Most towns in Holland had never joined the Hanseatic League, and consequently could not be bothered with its protectionist rules. Amsterdam now became its most serious rival, but Hoorn and Enkhuizen also prospered.

The importance, but also the vulnerability of trade to the Baltic was revealed by the famine that struck the Netherlands when the passage through the Danish Sound was closed between 1531 and 1537, as a result of a war of succession in Denmark. It had been a long time since people in Holland had been able to survive on the produce of their own land, only, having grown in numbers and having specialized in fishing, trade and industry. Consequently, they now had to rely on large stores of grain, or increase the agricultural surface to feed more mouths. Of course, problems were less acute in the mostly agricultural inland states, which, moreover, were less densely populated.

Rather than agriculture, sea fishing had become increasingly important to the towns of Holland. The discovery, at the end of the fourteenth century, of the curing of herring, which enabled the fishermen to salt and preserve it aboard, led to a veritable herring industry. As a result, the related shipbuilding industry started to flourish again, too.

During the fifteenth century, a number of older industries continued to grow. Leiden and Haarlem became the leading centres in the manufacture of cloth from English wool. Beer was brewed in large quantities at Delft, Gouda, Haarlem and Amersfoort, some of it for export. Even the pope was said to prefer Dutch beer.

As most of these industries were town-based, Holland's rural areas were at a disadvantage in this prospering economy. As the towns were increasingly important to the count, now the duke of Burgundy, given their tax potential, he had to grant their demands for certain privileges. Also, simply to protect their own economic interests, towns tried to have some forms of countryside industry forbidden. Inevitably this led to the further growth of the towns, to the further urbanization of Holland.

However, the process also resulted in the origin of a fairly extensive proletariat in some of the larger industrial cities, due to the influx of penurious people from the agricultural regions.

All in all, by 1500, the state of Holland had taken the lead in the economy of the Northern Netherlands; this was to have a marked effect on politics in the centuries that followed.

11   Culture (1300–1550): the emergence of new trends

Renaissance and Humanism

Between 1300 and 1550, all over Europe changes took place in, mostly, elite culture, which deeply influenced the way Europeans looked at themselves and at their world. Gradually, educated people, the reading public, began to ask what was the status of the knowledge sanctioned by and transmitted through the agencies of the Church. Especially man's relationship to God and to the cosmos, God's creation, was now studied from a more empirical point of view. Not only texts, first of all THE text, the Bible, but also the 'book of nature' served as sources to be critically perused, to enable man to form his own opinions, and thus fulfil his duty to be really human.

In the Netherlands, this Humanism found its greatest champion in Desiderius Erasmus of Rotterdam (1469-1536). This scholar, already famous in his own day, applied the Humanist principle of studying the Classics, both religious and secular, in their original text to the study of Holy Scripture. Thus, he published the first scholarly edition of the Greek version of the New Testament, showing that the Latin one, long used, had been corrupted by ages of manuscript copying.

Erasmus's views on ethics and religion were akin to the spirit of the Modern Devotion. He believed in tolerance and peace, advocating a pure and sober form of religion, but within the context of the Roman Catholic Church, despite his own and others' growing criticism of its administrative and moral practices.

The Renaissance is traditionally linked to Humanism, of which it is the more visible expression, showing itself in new forms of architecture, sculpture and painting, but also of music and literature. Basically, European art now was inspired both by the (re-)discovery of the art of the ancient Romans and Greeks and by the idea that man should emulate and represent nature as best he could. Originating in Italy, the Renaissance, too, spread to the North, although, there, the various visual arts long retained their earlier, Gothic forms.

Desiderius Erasmus (1466–1536), depicted by Hans Holbein, the younger, ca 1523

Education and literature

Many Dutch Humanists were able to propound their ideas to a large audience because they taught at the Latin schools. These gradually became the leading educational institutions in the Netherlands. Originally, they were attached to the parish churches, and specifically served to train prospective clergy. As the urban population grew more affluent, they too began to show an interest in education. Often, town councils would demand a say in the governing of these schools, or established new ones. In the sixteenth century the schools administrated by the town were eclipsed by private schools. The authorities reacted by imposing fines, or by banning some subjects from the curriculum. Girls were sometimes admitted

The Latin School at Nijmegen, built in 1544–1545

to these private schools but not to the town schools.

Under the influence of Humanism, these schools, also named grammar schools or 'gymnasiums', came to stress the study of the Classics, and related subjects, though arithmetic, history and physics were part of the curriculum as well.

All in all, in the Netherlands educational establishments both for the rich and the poor soon exceeded both in quantity and quality what was offered in most other European countries. Consequently, the literacy rate rose. From the sixteenth century onwards, the comparatively low percentage of illiterate Dutch people never failed to astonish foreign visitors.

Obviously, this development would not have taken place if printing had not been invented in the middle of the fifteenth century. Though by now the German Johannes Gutenberg is credited with it, the Dutch for long tried to prove that Haarlem-born Laurens Janszoon Coster was the first to experiment with moveable type and should be given pride of place.

However this may be, printing started a cultural revolution of enormous impact. As prices for texts slowly dropped, a far larger public now could buy and read books for themselves and profitably attend school. Communication increased, and knowledge spread, and people slowly became aware of a wider world. Also, education and printing stimulated cultural participation in larger groups of the population. The well-to-do burghers took up literature, which always had been an aristocratic pastime. Merchants, bankers and entrepreneurs now formed 'chambers of rhetoric' where they studied poetry. There was a shift from chivalrous poetry towards dramatic art during the sixteenth century, as plays with a clear moral message became more popular. In the process, people felt the need to standardize spelling and to lay down rules for proper grammar and syntax. Slowly, modern Dutch was born.

Architecture, sculpture and painting

Wealthy townspeople also began to take an active interest in architecture. They frequently built their houses of stone, first using the new Gothic style, and, from the sixteenth century onwards, introducing Renaissance elements. Also, they contributed generously to the building of magnificent churches and town halls. Cities such as Amersfoort, Rhenen, Delft and Breda vied with each other in the construction of huge steeples, sometimes over a 100 metres tall. Mostly, these were attached to the town's main church, showing that religion and politics were closely connected.

Hieronymus Bosch (1450–1516), the 'Hay Wain', central panel, painted ca 1515.
It is an allegory of man's need for material gratification that will, inevitably, lead him to Hell

Before c. 1550, sculpture and painting was usually inspired and commissioned by the aristocracy and the clergy. But the burghers, too, began to pay for religious art. Again, this has its background in the close connection between socio-economic and religious life. Economic life in the towns was dominated by guilds, i.e. groups representing a specific profession, like the bakers' guild or the butchers' guild. Social life was centred around and in fraternities, instituted to take care of all kinds social services, such as paying for the members' burials, doling out alms to the poor, et cetera. These aspects of life all were celebrated in the town's churches. There, sumptuous guild and fraternity chapels were constructed, or at the least a special altar was erected. Both chapels and altars were adorned with sculpted and painted images of the saints specifically venerated by the group who paid for them. The most famous fifteenth-century sculptor was Adriaen van Wesel, from Utrecht (c.1420-1500), who created an altar to the Virgin Mary in St. James's church at 's Hertogenbosch for the 'Illustrious Fraternity of Our Lady'.

Together with a few of its smaller neighbouring towns, Utrecht had been the cultural heart of the Netherlands since about 1400. Both the bishops and the mostly aristocratic canons of the five chapters employed numerous skilled artists. Miniature painting blossomed here in the first half of the fifteenth century. The 'Book of Hours' made c. 1430 for Catherine of Cleves, wife of Duke Arnold of Gelderland, is the best known example of this art. Miniature painting at Utrecht differed from that of the Southern Netherlands by its realism and the choice of subjects from everyday life, characteristics which continued to prevail in Dutch art for centuries to come.

Non-religious painting, which had hardly existed before 1400, first appeared near Utrecht, too, and then in Gouda, Oudewater and Schoonhoven. The earliest known Dutch portrait, showing the Lady Lijsbeth van Duvenvoirde, was painted on parchment in 1430.

From the second half of the fifteenth century onwards, the economic prosperity of the towns of Holland also stimulated painting. Soon, Haarlem became a new cultural centre, attracting artists from Utrecht such as Albert van Ouwater. Well-known members of the Haarlem school of artists were Geertgen tot Sint Jans (c. 1467-1495) and Diederik Bouts (c. 1475), who later moved to Louvain.

During the first half of the sixteenth century, the Renaissance style became visible not only in architecture but also in painting and sculpture. Basically, many artists now felt that to survive in a highly competitive market and produce work that represented the height of fashion, they had to travel to Italy, the cradle of Humanism and the Renaissance. The first artist known to have made the trip was Jan Gossaert, who worked at the court of the Utrecht bishop David of Burgundy. His pupil Jan van Scorel (1495-1562), well known for his portraits and religious works, followed in his steps. Other painters working in the new style were, for example, Lucas van Leyden (1494-1533), famous in his own day for his portraits and altarpieces,

The great tower of Utrecht cathedral, started in 1321 and finished in 1382. It is shown here in a 19th-century lithograph

and especially for his engravings. This new form of art had come with the invention of printing and soon was in great demand by the burgher class, if only because woodcuts and copper engravings were less expensive that oil paintings.

The artist Hieronymus Bosch (1450-1516) worked in Brabant, principally at 's Hertogenbosch. Some people maintain that the spirit of the Middle Ages still shows strong in his unusually visionary work, inspired perhaps by the misery of contemporary rural life and the persecution of witchcraft just now beginning. This may be true, for while a new age was dawning, the earlier culture lingered on.

Luther and Calvin

In fifteenth-century religion, enthusiasm for the sober life-style preached by the Modern Devotion-movement had waned. There now was a growing demand for pomp and ceremony, in festive processions and ostentatious pilgrimages. At the same time, wealthy citizens increasingly asked friars from the so-called mendicant Orders to settle in their towns. They felt they were fulfilling their religious duties by donating money to these monks who advocated an unworldly way of life.

Anonymous 17th-century allegorical painting showing 'Peace pleading for tolerance between the Churches'. At the table are seated: Calvin, the Pope, Luther and an Anabaptist
RMA

Also in the fifteenth century a religious revival arose in the German countries, with preachers advocating a return to a purer faith. For people came to abhor the many malpractices which, far from being discouraged, were openly tolerated by the Church of Rome. Yearning for ways to express a stronger, more personal belief and also condemning the accumulation of ecclesiastical dignities, the sale of Church offices and of so-called letters of indulgence (basically documents that granted forgiveness for one's sins in return for payment of a certain sum), in 1517 Martin Luther decided to publish his reformist ideas in his famous 95 theses. Thus, another reformation movement started. Though it certainly was not the first ever, it proved to be by far the most successful, if only because its ideas could be spread all over Europe by means of the new communication medium, the printed text. Consequently, we now refer to it as 'The' Reformation.

Luther's ideas soon found favour in the Netherlands. However, Habsburg central government was opposed to religious variety if only because it fostered political unrest. In 1521, Brussels issued the first edict against the Reformers, or Protestants. Already in 1525 it ordered Jan de Bakker to be burnt at Woerden, to set an example. This stern policy resulted from the fact that by now a movement far more aggressive than peace-loving Lutheranism had risen in southern Germany, appealing to the lower classes in particular. Known as Anabaptism, and promising equal rights to all its members, it spread rapidly over north-western Europe. Jan Beukels of Leiden, one of the leading Anabaptists in the Netherlands, even led the conquest of the German city of Munster, where the movement then maintained a 'Kingdom of God' for almost a year. Everywhere, the followers of this revolutionary group were persecuted fiercely by the authorities, especially after a failed attempt to set up a similar community in Amsterdam. Anabaptism is not to be confused with the Baptist movement that was also persecuted, although it was of a more peaceable nature. This sect had many followers in Friesland where it was preached by Menno Simons - hence their name Mennonites. Last, but not least, the Reformation manifested itself in the Calvinist movement, named after John Calvin, who preached his ideas in Geneva. Though his doctrine did not spread widely in the Netherlands before 1550, in subsequent decades it became the foremost Protestant force, there.

Charles V favoured severe action against Protestantism in all his states, and, moreover, felt he needed a strong Church to counter its consequences, a Church which he could dominate. Therefore, as early as 1522 he consulted with the pope on a reorganization of the episcopal sees, to make Church policy more bureaucratically efficient and, also, subservient to his own administrative interests. However, most of his subjects saw this as another intolerable example of Habsburg centralizing power that undermined the independence of the Netherlands' states. Therefore Church reorganization was not realized during Charles's rule. Meanwhile, with religious conflict turning into outright religious wars all over Europe, the Emperor did seek to solve the problems. In 1555, a 'peace of religion'-treaty was signed at Augsburg. It decreed that in each of the dozens of principalities that formed the vast Holy Roman Empire, the religion of the ruler was to be accepted by his subjects. This meant that the seventeen states of the Netherlands would be obliged to remain Roman Catholic, since that was the faith of the Emperor Charles, their ruler, and even more so of his son and successor, King Philip II of Spain.

The execution of the heretic Anabaptists on the Amsterdam Dam Square, in 1535. Engraving by J. van Gensel
GAA

12 Society and politics after c. 1550: growing opposition to 'Spanish' rule

In 1549, Charles V issued the so-called 'Pragmatic Sanction'. In this document, he decreed that a single law of inheritance would be followed in all the seventeen Netherlands, ensuring they would pass as an indivisible entity to the successor of the ruling prince, who was to be confirmed by the Holy Roman Emperor as the Netherlands' suzerain. The assemblies of the seventeen states duly ratified the Sanction, after which Philip, Charles's son, made his solemn entry in the Netherlands to be honoured as his father's successor in all of them. He toured the seventeen capitals, being received with grand processions, banquets and other civic ritual. It was an occasion for a great display of propagandistic art, all serving to proclaim his right to rule by divine law. At the same time, the regional elites, in the very act of accepting Philip's rule, yet tried to assert their continued role in state government by asking him to confirm their privileges.

King Philip II (1527–1598)

In 1555, Philip took over from his father and Charles retired to a Spanish monastery where he died three years later. Also in 1555, Charles's governor-general in the Netherlands, Mary of Hungary, had left her post. For as long as Philip resided in the Netherlands, mainly to supervise the ongoing Habsburg war with France, he was able to govern in person.

The administration continued as before, with the Council of State as the main royal advisory body in name, now headed by Antoine Perrenot de Granvelle, who was later named cardinal. He, the most influential civil servant, was assisted by five senior legal officials. Moreover, the Council comprised a number of major aristocrats, including the Counts of Lalaing and of Egmond, as well as William of Nassau, who stemmed from one of the Empire's leading noble families, but also owned extensive properties in the Netherlands, as well as having inherited the sovereign principality of Orange, a tiny but independent state south of France.

However, King Philip, rather than ruling with these magnates, who controlled enor-

Philip II (1527–1598), lord of each of the seventeen, independent Netherlands, and king of Spain, by Antonio Moro, c. 1554

William, count of
Nassau, prince of
Orange (1533–1584), as
a young man, depicted
ca 1545 by Cornelis
Anthonisz.
Rijksprentenkabinet

mous estates and, consequently, had a great hold over the common people, preferred to consult a few trusted advisors, only. Thus disregarded, the majority of the mighty nobles in the Council of State found the situation extremely frustrating. So did the Prince of Orange, the more so as he had been a favourite at the court of Charles V. Though he had befriended Cardinal Granvelle, he fell from grace when, in 1561, against Granvelle's advice, he married Anna of Saxony, the protestant and very wealthy daughter of one of Charles's old enemies in the German Empire.

Cardinal Granvelle

When Philip left the Netherlands in 1559, Granvelle gradually assumed effective power, to the displeasure of Margaretha of Parma, the king's half-sister, who now ruled in her brother's place. In the mean time, several of the major nobles had been named the king's lieutenants, or 'stadhouders' in each of the seventeen states, now increasingly called provinces, as if to indicate that their erstwhile independence was a thing of the past.

Among them was William of Orange, who was given the lord-lieuten-antship of Holland, Zeeland, West-Friesland and Utrecht. Yet, Granvelle increasingly sought to exclude the nobles from the consultations of the Council of State. Moreover, there was another way in which he was able to influence central government. In 1559, the long-awaited reorganization of Church hierarchy in the Netherlands had been effectuated. All new dioceses were placed under the supervision of the archbishop of Mechlin, who also became the spokesman for the clergy in the States of Brabant. Formerly this had been a privilege of the abbot of the great monastery of Afflighem. In view of its enormous wealth, this abbey had been 'incorporated' in the diocese, thus losing its independence but enabling the archbishop to enjoy the privileges of the abbot. The newly-appointed archbishop of Mechlin was none other than Granvelle himself, who now acquired a double hold on the government of the Netherlands.

Anonymous portrait of Antoine Perrenot de Granvelle (1517–1586), cardinal and chief minister of Charles V and Phillip II, c. 1565
RMA

The League of the Noblemen:
the Prince of Orange and other magnates

In 1562, the dissatisfied court nobles formed a league under the leadership of William of Orange. They demanded that the King dismiss Granvelle. They succeeded because Margaretha had her own reservations about the Cardinal's performance. The King gave in. In 1564, on the pretext of a family visit, Granvelle left the Netherlands, never to return.

While his departure gave the nobles more influence in central government, they were not satisfied, yet, because by now the seventeen states were in the throes of an economic depression. This was partly a result of the costly wars waged Europe-wide by Charles V, which Philip II was continuing. To finance his campaigns, Charles had borrowed heavily at high rates of interest. Though Spain provided the Netherlands with funds from the proceeds of its South-American gold and silver, the Dutch were nevertheless convinced that their tax moneys were often used in wars which were of no importance to them, but only served the aggrandizement of the Habsburg family in far-away places of Europe and the overseas world. As under Philip's and Granvelle's rule taxes rose dramatically, fiscal policy elicited increasing protest. The King's attempts to introduce a capital levy on trade and industry were rejected resolutely by the States-General. After all, the representatives of the cities often were businessmen themselves.

The first signs of rebellion

Since 1563, the economic situation had been deteriorating even further for most of the population. The Danish Sound was closed yet again during a war between Sweden and Denmark. Both merchant shipping and transports of grain from the Baltic, a lifeline of food, became impossible. When the harvest also failed, after an unusually severe winter, people were on the verge of rebellion, the more so as they had other grievances as well.

As all over Europe, occasional uprisings were not at all unusual in the Netherlands. During the long period of the seventeen states' independence most cities had gained privileges which they intended to keep. If these were threatened, a town often would rise in revolt against the duke or count who usually was obliged to give in if only because he could not afford to antagonize his tax-paying burghers.

One of these regional privileges was the administration of justice. Consequently, in most of the seventeen Netherlands, people had come to object to such central jurisdictional bodies as the Parliament of Mechlin. However, they positively hated the Inquisition set up by Charles V to deal with the persecution of the Protestants, considered to be heretics, and with other dissidents. Although in most states the ruling elites were well aware that religious differences caused trouble, they felt persecution by the central government fundamentally harmed their own authority. Also, they were filled with dismay seeing their fellow people being deported to be tortured or burned at the stake in Brussels. As a result, in Holland no heretics were burned after 1553 and the death sentence for heresy became rare in Friesland.

In the 1560's, the difficult financial and economic situation, combined with religious persecution and political unrest caused feelings to run high indeed. Moreover, from 1560 onwards the Protestants, partly Lutheran, partly Calvinist, had established a more efficient organization. In this, they were influenced and strengthened by the large numbers of Calvinist refugees who had fled Roman Catholic France to escape religious persecution, there. These so-called Huguenots, who had well-organized communities themselves, now helped create these in the Netherlands, too. Within a few years the far stricter doctrines of John Calvin almost replaced the more moderate forms of Protestantism such as Lutheranism.

William of Orange, later nicknamed the Silent, became leader of the revolt in the Netherlands.
Portrait attributed to Adriaen Key, c. 1579
RVD Den Haag

The 'Compromise' of the minor nobles

Calvinism recruited followers among all ranks of the population. A number of the lesser nobility also sympathized with it or even joined its local communities. Like the court grandees, these minor nobles were dissatisfied with the way central government operated. Many felt their privileged position was undermined, both economically and militarily, what with heavy taxation and the introduction of mercenary armies, which robbed them of lucrative positions in the military. Like the court nobles, they decided to co-operate and soon formed their own league called the "Compromise". They then proceeded to present the royal governor-general, Margaretha, with a petition asking her to abolish the Inquisition. While this was an action aimed at a hated symbol, their having embraced Calvinism could be interpreted as a sign of revolt. Signed by over 400 minor nobles, the petition was delivered by 200 armed men on the 5th of April, 1566. Obviously, Margaretha and her councillors were less than pleased. Yet, Berlaymont, a member of the Council of State, is reported to have said, rather disparagingly because, perhaps, he underestimated the danger of the situation, that these men were beggars only, or 'gueux' in French. The nobles were quick to adopt the Dutch form, proudly calling themselves 'geuzen'.

Two of the most influential court nobles, the lords of Montigny and Bergen, now travelled to Spain to present the petition to the King himself. For while Margaretha had felt forced to not reject the nobles' request, promising that no one would be persecuted for his beliefs, her decision yet had to meet with the King's approval.

Still, Margaretha's promise did not satisfy the staunch Calvinists who also wanted the freedom to worship openly. As a form of provocation, they began to organize open-air religious meetings, which sometimes were attended by over a thousand people. Soon, those who attended these services decided to go well-armed, to be able to defend themselves against government officials. This, of course, was felt to be another provocation by the authorities, for such actions turned these meetings into political, rather more than religious manifestations. Inevitably, an atmosphere of rebellion and oppression soon prevailed.

The nobles offer their petition to the king's governor in the Netherlands
Atlas van Stolk

The iconoclast fury:
the destruction of the images

Meanwhile, rumour had it that some of the leading nobles had converted to the Reformation, too, thereby committing heresy and, consequently, becoming enemies of the state. Egmond, Hoorne and Orange were among those suspected. They announced their intention of leaving the Netherlands, to the displeasure of Margaretha, who sorely needed their authority to calm the Calvinist populace. Although she was successful in persuading them to stay for the time being, the storm could no longer be averted, especially in the South of Flanders, which was in the grip of a deep depression. There was general unrest, as a result of a shortage of food because now the Danish Sound had frozen over and again no grain arrived from the Baltics. Also, there was widespread unemployment in the textile industry due to the falling supply of wool from England. In August 1566, pent-up feelings erupted and an iconoclast fury broke out, causing irreparable damage in many churches. Especially, sculpted, painted and stained-glass representations of saints, and other symbols of the official Church, mainly hated because of its association with a repressive government, were destroyed, to prepare the churches for Protestant worship, which did not allow images.

Iconoclasm in the churches of the Netherlands, by D. van Delen. Unlike the many engraved representations, it is the only existing painted one (1630)

In these dire circumstances, Margaretha felt forced to granted the Calvinists permission to openly worship in those areas where they were already convening secretly. This satisfied the minor nobles who now promised to support her in maintaining order. Most of the major aristocrats also rallied to her.

The renewed oath of allegiance to King Philip

At the beginning of 1567, both the members of the famous Order of the Golden Fleece, which had been devised by the Burgundian dukes to foster some spirit of unity among the leading aristocracy of their many states, and the senior government officials and officers all were asked to renew their oath of allegiance to Philip II. However, some of the major nobles, including Orange and Hoorne, refused to do so. Hoorne later complied, but in May, when the situation deteriorated, the Prince of Orange fled to the German lands, together with thousands of other rebels, most of them Calvinists. At the same time, some of the most rebellious men, including many whose possessions had been confiscated, took to the sea, now to continue their actions as 'Sea Beggars'.

The Duke of Alba and the Council of Blood

At her wits' end, the governor-general resigned her post. Her rather panicky account of the situation led Philip to raise an army of 10,000 men who entered the Netherlands on 22 August 1567, led by Don Fernando Alvarez de Toledo, third Duke of Alba. The King had given Alba, a proven military leader, almost unlimited power to act as his new governor-general. One of the Duke's first decisions was to set up a 'Council of Troubles', soon commonly known as the 'Council of Blood', on account of the death sentences it pronounced. Alba himself, of course, soon was nick-named the 'Iron Duke'. The King's rigorous policy, prompted by exaggerated reports of the situation in his northern states, probably caused a substantial part of the Calvinist Dutch population finally to reject his authority, or rather that of his hated representatives.

William of Orange, or 'the Silent', as he now became known - because he used to keep his own counsel rather than trusting others -, also suffered personal loss at Alba's hands. His eldest son and heir, Prince Philip-William, named after the King, who was a student at Louvain, was abducted and subsequently held hostage in Spain, never to see his father again. Orange's fellow campaigners, Egmond and Hoorne, were taken prisoner, too, and even executed in 1568.

13 Decades of strife

1568: the beginning of a war that would last for 'eighty years'

Meanwhile, in the German countries, the Prince of Orange had raised four small armies of mercenaries that were to invade the Netherlands under his own leadership and that of his brothers, the three Counts of Nassau. In May, 1568, a battle was fought at Heiligerlee in Groningen, and Philip's stadhouder in Friesland was defeated, but Adolph of Nassau was killed. Two months later this small army, now led by Lodewijk of Nassau, was defeated, by Alba himself.

Prince William's own invasion of Brabant, in the autumn of 1568, also failed. He was compelled to retreat to Germany again, disbanding his armies due to lack of funds. When making his plans, Orange had counted on support from the people. But however rebellious their mood, they were still not desperate enough to follow the Prince in violently challenging the policies pursued in the King's sacred name. Whether Orange, at that time, had any other, more far-reaching plans, is uncertain.

The situation changed when, in addition to his persecution of the Calvinists, Alba introduced new tax measures. These met with widespread

The Battle of Heiligerlee (1568)
Atlas van Stolk

Graff Ludwich wie ein Khuener heldt. Zu Groningen sich gab ins feldt. — Da der von Arnbergh vnd seine bende. Von ihm erschlagen, vnd Zertrent. Anno Dñj. M. D. LXVIII. XXIIII Maij. — Sexstuck, geschutz sampt allehädt. Gelt, pferdt, wagen vnd Prouiandt. — Erobert hat zur selber frist. Graff Adolff auch erschlage ist

opposition although they actually were very sensible, aiming at a more proportional distribution of the fiscal burden over the population. Especially merchants and entrepreneurs, the urban elite, objected to Alba's plan to levy a sales' tax of 10% on all transactions, known as the 'Tenth Penny'. Besides the blow this would deal to business, it would also weaken the power of the purse of the States-General and thus its leverage with the government, because these fiscal measures were meant to be permanent.

Although the States-General bought off their obligation to pay the 'Tenth Penny' for the first two year period, in 1571 Alba made a fresh attempt to levy the tax, albeit in a milder form. He now met with resistance not only from many town councils, but also from such a hitherto loyal member of the Council of State as Berlaymont. At this point Alba resigned, but the King asked him not to leave before he had restored law and order.

One of the 'water beggars', William van der Marck, lord of Lumey, depicted as conqueror of the town of Den Briel, 1572

1572: the capture of the town of Brill

Meanwhile, William of Orange had realized that he might as well profit from the growing opposition, and had raised a new army, with the support of the French Protestants who were more than willing to combat their archenemies, the Spaniards. However, his plan to attack the government troops from the South and the East failed miserably. The 'Watergeuzen', or Sea Beggars, who were campaigning to occupy some of the important coastal towns of Holland and Zeeland, were more successful. On the first of April, 1572, they captured Brill - Den Briel, or Brielle -, in the same month taking Veere and Vlissingen - Flushing - as well. At last, the revolt the Prince had hoped for so long did erupt in Holland, where he still claimed to be the King's lieutenant. Most of the towns rallied to his side, with a few exceptions, including Amsterdam that feared for its commercial interests. Meanwhile, since Alba was campaigning against an army once more commanded by Lodewijk of Nassau in the South, he was unable to crush the revolt.

An assembly of the rebel towns convened at Dordrecht and now elected William of Orange as 'stadhouder', suggesting that he still formally represented the King's authority. In doing so, they tried to uphold the fiction that the King, of course, was well-intentioned towards his seventeen Netherlands, but that his representatives in Brussels were misinforming him, thus causing him to endorse bad policies. Actually, at first, the rebels did not intend to withdraw their allegiance to the King - though they eventually proceeded to do so. They only demanded that their rights and privileges be acknowledged and that the interests of the Netherlands would no longer be subservient to Spanish policy. In the *Wilhelmus van Nassouwe*, a

Als der Prins vber den Rhein voihr
Nitt weit zu Duysburg von der Roihr

Hatt er sein volck nidergeschlagen
Vor Romund mitt man.roß.vnd wagē

Die Statt sich nitt ergeben wult
Darumb der Prins war ir nitt hult

Anno Dñi. M. D. LXXII. IIII. Auguſt:

Anonymous engraving, showing William of Orange laying siege to the town of Roermond in July 1572
Gemeentearchief Roermond

popular battle song written at this time (which only in the twentieth century was promoted to the status of Dutch National Anthem), William's own words were given as: 'I have always honoured the King of Spain'.

Yet, it could hardly be denied that a revolt had started. Indeed, it spread from Holland to the other provinces. Parts of Friesland and Gelderland even were won for the Prince. But the Massacre of St. Bartholomew's Eve in Paris, on 24 August 1572, during which countless Huguenots were murdered by their Catholic countrymen, put an end to French support. Without financial aid from France, William of Orange was forced once more to disband his army. He withdrew to Holland, the province which had been the first to support him.

1573 and 1574: the relief of Alkmaar and Leiden

Alba took his revenge by sending an army to plunder some of the rebellious towns. Laying siege to Alkmaar, the Spanish troops yet had to retreat, for water, so often the enemy of the Dutch, came to the rebels' rescue now. By cutting the dykes, they inundated the land surrounding the town. This forced the Spanish army to leave. The event, which took place on the 8th of October, 1573, is still celebrated as the first rebel victory.

Skirmishes continued, though. A year later, on 3 October 1574, Leiden was taken by the rebels, who succeeded to hold it. In 1575, to thank God, the first university of the northern Netherlands was founded there, for the purpose of training Protestant ministers. Meanwhile, the Prince of Orange formally had joined the Calvinist Church. Moreover, at least in Holland the tide had turned to such an extent that the provincial States now prohibited Roman Catholic worship altogether, which inevitably created fear amongst the Roman Catholics who were sympathetic to the rebel cause.

Anonymous portrait of Don Juan of Austria (1547–1578), regent of the Netherlands (1576–1578)
RMA

1576: the Pacification of Ghent

Don Luis de Requesens, appointed governor-general after the departure of Alba in 1573, attempted to reach an agreement with the rebellious leaders of Holland at a conference in Breda, but without success. He died suddenly in 1576, after which the Spanish troops, who had not been paid for some time, advanced on the wealthy provinces of Brabant and Flanders. They brutalized the population, looting and raiding the countryside and threatening the towns. With royal, Spanish authority temporarily absent, the Council of State now took the reins of government. In defiance of the King, the States-General were convened at Ghent where a peace treaty between the contending provinces was signed.

In this 'Pacification of Ghent', the seventeen provinces pledged to co-operate to end the 'Spanish Fury'. Thus, the Netherlands were united against Spanish politics and the perceived brutality of Spanish methods, which continued with the arrival of a new royal governor-general, Prince John of Austria. However, no definite solution was found for the growing religious differences. Admittedly, part of the Ghent-agreement was that persecution of the Protestants, the 'heretics', was to be suspended but that, also, Catholics - outside Holland and Zeeland - were to be left in peace. Seemingly, the ideal of tolerance, which Orange, according to some historians, always had cherished, seemed to have been achieved, if only partially. Yet, to what extent the various states really were willing to accept equality of religions was unclear or, rather, soon became very clear indeed.

1579: the Union of Arras and the Union of Utrecht

Meanwhile, rebellion now gained ground in the southern Netherlands as well. William of Orange even entered Brussels in triumph. But a number of nobles resisted the rise of Calvinism and joined forces under the leadership of Montigny. They formed the Union of Arras or Atrecht on the 6th of January, 1579. Actually, this was a declaration of allegiance to King

Title-page and first page
of the 'Act of Abjuration'
that severed the link
between the Northern
Netherlands and Philip II,
printed at Leiden 1581

Philip and to the Roman Catholic Church. In reaction, on the 23rd of January, 1579, the Union of Utrecht was proclaimed. It was a pact between a number of the northern provinces, aiming to continue the struggle against Spain. It was signed by Holland, Zeeland, Utrecht and by the countryside regions of Groningen. William's brother, Count John of Nassau, signed for Gelderland. Yet, the Guelders' town of Zutphen only joined after some hesitation. Later, the regions of Drenthe and Overijssel acceded to the Union as well. They all agreed that the participating states were to remain united in a 'perpetual' alliance, and 'as if they were one', but that, on the other hand, each state was to retain its historically acquired rights. Important decisions such as declarations of war or treaties of peace and the introduction of tax measures were only valid if taken unanimously. In religious matters, each state had the right to decide for itself, although it was understood there was to be no further religious persecution.

1581: the 'Act of Abjuration': the seven Northern Netherlands declare their independence from Spain

Almost inevitably, William of Orange, who supported the Union though the project was initiated mainly by his brother John, was formally outlawed by Philip in 1580. Consequently, the Prince advised the States-General to elect a new sovereign, suggesting the French king's brother, the Duke of Anjou. Indeed, nor William, nor the other rebels yet could envisage a state or, as in this case, a confederation of states which would not have their own ruler, as was normal in almost all other states of Europe. Moreover, in selecting Anjou, he hoped to again engage French support against Spain. However, declaring he himself would continue to hold power in Holland and Zeeland, he was perhaps less sure of the final outcome.

The natural sequel to this transfer of sovereignty was the 'Act of Abjuration' of the 22nd of July 1581. In it, the States-General of the seven provinces, now assembled at The Hague, formally withdrew their allegiance from Philip II. Anjou's appointment soon proved a symbolic act, only. In fact, government was in the hands of William of Orange and the rebellious States-General. The various states, or provinces, retaining their sovereignty, now were to be governed by their Provincial States, a body elected from the nobility and the urban bourgeoisie.

1584: the assassination of William of Orange

On 10 July 1584, Prince William was assassinated at Delft, at the age of 51, by a man called Balthasar Gerards. The bullet hole is still shown in the 'Prinsenhof', the former monastery where William had taken up residence. With him, the Dutch Revolt had lost its by now natural leader. This may well have taught the provinces united in the Union of Utrecht to pull together even more firmly. For the time being, the States-General decided to entrust a Council of State with the confederation's central government. Prince Maurice, William's seventeen year-old second son, was made a member.

In Friesland, however, Count John of Nassau, the son of one of William's brothers, was elected to be the new stadhouder.

All the time, the idea that a state could manage without a personal sovereign still was alien to the leading politicians. For this reason, on the death of Anjou, sovereignty was offered first to the king of France himself, who refused it, and then to Queen Elizabeth of England, who was waging her own war against Spain. However, she only promised to send someone suitable for the position of governor-general. Her choice fell on her then favourite, the Earl of Leicester, who was appointed in 1586. However, his overbearing attitude during his two year-stay in the Netherlands did not impress the new leaders, least so the young, but ambitious Prince Maurice. Leicester soon felt forced to return to England.

After his departure, the future for the budding confederation looked bleaker than ever. In Autumn, 1588, a huge Spanish fleet, an armada which King Philip thought 'invincible', was plying its way to the Netherlands to crush the rebellion once and for all and to also teach England a lesson. Fortunately for the rebel provinces, the Armada was defeated off the coast of England and its remnants were almost completely destroyed by storm.

(Left) The stairs where, in 1584, William collapsed when he was hit by his assassin's bullet

(Right) Tomb of William of Orange, in the New Church at Delft (1623). In the crypt underneath, most members of the Orange-Nassau family have been buried

14 The 'Republic of the Seven United Provinces' on its way to independence

Prince Maurice and Johan van Oldenbarnevelt

It was mainly due to the efforts of two emerging key figures, Prince Maurice of Orange and Johan van Oldenbarnevelt, that the 'ad hoc' independent union of the seven Netherlands survived as a permanent state. Oldenbarnevelt (1547-1619) was the grand pensionary, or senior administrator, of the province of Holland; authorized to sign resolutions on its behalf, he was in fact this mini-state's chief policy maker. Soon after the death of William the Silent, he persuaded the States of Holland to elect Prince Maurice as stadhouder: an increasingly bizarre construction, for by now the person whose place the Prince was supposed to hold, King Philip of Spain, had been formally abjured. In fact, one must assume that the fiction prevailed that Maurice somehow personified, embodied, the authority of the actual, but collective and anonymous sovereign, the elected provincial States themselves.

This anomaly indicates that, on the one hand, there existed a growing awareness that the Northern Netherlands were a confederation of seven tiny republics which, however, in international parlance now came to be called the 'Republic of the Seven United Dutch Provinces', for dealing with seven separate little states was beyond the capacity of European political and diplomatic life. On the other hand, these seven united states still needed someone to exercise a number of quasi-monarchical tasks, without, however, having any real monarchical authority or power. Who could do so better than the son of William the Silent, who was increasingly revered as the Republic's founding father? Moreover, Prince Maurice proved a very competent military leader and as such much needed to lead the new Republic's soldiers in their continuing war with Spain. He soon assumed the function of captain-general of the entire Republic's army. In the ongoing campaigns, he won many battles, assisted by his cousin William Louis, who had succeeded his father as stadhouder of Friesland.

Maurice's military progress came to a halt in 1595, when the States-General lacked funds to pay the troops. But in 1596 both France and England, for political reasons of their own, were at last prepared to support the United Provinces and even to acknowledge them as an independent federation that could act on the international stage. In June of the same year, Van Oldenbarnevelt succeeded in uniting the Northern Netherlands with France and England in the Triple Alliance.

The Twelve Years' Truce 1609-1621

In the year of his death, 1598, Philip II granted those states of the former seventeen Netherlands that had remained faithful to him to his daughter Isabella, on the occasion of her marriage to the new governor-general, her cousin Archduke Albert of Austria. In Spain the climate was ripe for

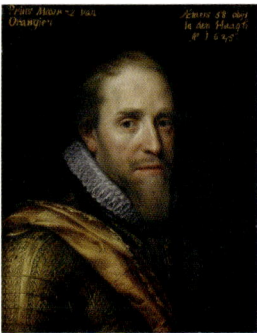

Anonymous portrait of Maurits of Nassau, prince of Orange (1567–1625)
RMA

a change of policy towards the Netherlands: the government in Madrid began to realize that it simply lacked the financial resources to pay for an interminable succession of expensive annual military campaigns; specifically the interest on the sums borrowed for this purpose was crippling the treasury.

In the breakaway northern provinces, two trends in dealing with Spain gradually emerged. One was for continuing efforts to win over the remaining ten Netherlands, now mostly called the Southern Netherlands although even the word 'Belgium' did exist already, to the cause of the revolt. The other was satisfied with the status quo.

Prince Maurice definitely led the first group. Admittedly, he had his own, partly self-interested reasons for wanting to continue the war. As stadhouder, he was but the servant of the five states which had appointed him - the other two having opted for his cousin. His one position of real power was that of captain-general of the Union. Without a war, this title would lose its meaning and the prince would lose much of his power, also his power of patronage, for he was entitled to nominate his favourites as commanding officers in the army.

Oldenbarnevelt led those who argued the Dutch badly needed to conclude peace with Spain. In this, he represented the views of most of the authorities in the towns of Holland. These 'regents' usually came from leading merchant families. They felt the war was creating ever bigger financial problems. Nor did they see any gain in an alliance with the southern provinces, particularly Flanders with its wealthy trading towns. Trade and industry were just beginning to prosper in the northern Netherlands, partly as a result of their decline in the south due to the blockade of the Scheldt River, that used to be the lifeline of Amsterdam's greatest competitor, Antwerp. To continue this situation would have to be a fundamental condition of any peace treaty. Yet, there also were merchants who favoured the war which had brought them prosperity. Moreover, Calvinist zealots, such as the ministers of the Protestant Church, but merchants and ordinary people as well, also advocated continuing the struggle against Catholic Spain, in the Catholic South. To them, Roman Catholicism, or popery, was the work of the Devil.

In 1609, Oldenbarnevelt succeeded in concluding a Twelve Years' Truce with Isabella and Albert, obviously against the wish of Prince Maurice. There were to be no hostilities during this period and the status quo was to be maintained, both in Europe and abroad, in America and Asia, or: the East Indies, where the two camps had been competing as well. On behalf of King Philip III of Spain, the Archduke and his wife also agreed to acknowledge the sovereignty of the Republic, at least for the duration of the truce.

Grand Pensionary Johan van Oldenbarnevelt (1547–1619), who effectively ruled the Dutch Republic during the first decades of the 17th century
Atlas van Stolk

Arminians and Gomarians

The opposing political views held by Maurice and Oldenbarnevelt at the beginning of the Twelve Years' Truce were aggravated by religious differences within the Calvinist community. In 1603, a certain Protestant minister, Arminius, had been named professor of theology at Leiden. He held

Franciscus Gomarus
(1563-1641)

fairly liberal views, particularly on the much-discussed tenet of predestination, a cornerstone of Calvinist doctrine which holds that salvation is foreordained by God for some and not for others. It was not long before Arminius came into conflict with Gomarus, also a Leiden professor, who held equally strong but opposing views on this vital issue. The two theologians soon found a following both among their fellow ministers and among the faithful. In 1610, a year after the death of Arminius, one of his followers presented a 'remonstrance' against predestination to the States-General; this may seem a strange action, but one has to remember that the Calvinist Church did and does not have a supreme ecclesiastical authority who might order a binding ruling on such dogmatic issues. The 'remonstrance' was reciprocated with a 'counter-remonstrance' from the Gomarians in 1611.

The States-General, who feared religious differences in the seven provinces, ordered the two parties to convene for a conference. However, they would not be reconciled. Over the following years, the conflict deepened, with Oldenbarnevelt supporting the tolerant Remonstrants (the moderates), and Prince Maurice taking the side of the Counter Remonstrants (the strictly orthodox). The States of Holland chose the side of Oldenbarnevelt and the Remonstrants, relieved as they were that this group acknowledged temporal authority as the supreme power in religious matters as well. However, this stance did not suit the city council of Amsterdam which remained orthodox to demonstrate its political independence to the other towns of Holland.

The Synod of Dordtrecht 1618-1619

Oldenbarnevelt increasingly felt that civil government should indeed have the last say in religious matters if it were to avoid great political and social unrest. Consequently, in 1617 the States of Holland passed the 'sharp resolution', refusing to convene a national synod to deal with the problems for fear that the other six provinces would use this religious issue as a pretext to voice their increasing uneasiness over Holland's growing economic and political preponderance in the federation. If the other states united on this point, they might continue to subject Holland to their political will.

The Grand Pensionary also advised the town councils of Holland to employ a force of "waardgelders", or mercenaries, to deal with rioters. As these troops were to replace the regular militia led by Prince Maurice, he interpreted Oldenbarnevelt's policy as a direct attack on his authority as captain-general. This exacerbated the distrust which had started to grow between the two a decade earlier, when truce with Spain had been concluded against Maurice's will.

Not unexpectedly, the majority of the other provinces in the States-General took the side of the Prince against the overbearing state of Holland. In 1618, it was decided to hold a national synod after all, which then met at Dordrecht. The Remonstrant doctrines were denounced and Calvinist orthodoxy was formulated for all to adhere to. A new translation of the Bible, to establish an unequivocal foundation for theological truth, was

The Synod of Dordrecht (1618), where representatives of the Reformed Churches in
the Northern Netherlands tried to restore religious unity

Atlas van Stolk

Prince Maurice and his
half-brother, Prince
Frederic-Henry, riding
out from the erstwhile
palace of the counts of
Holland at The Hague,
1627
RMA

also ordered. Completed in 1637, it was called the 'States' Bible'. For many Dutch Protestants it represented the only true version of God's Word until well into the twentieth century. Also, for many children it was the one text from which they were taught proper Dutch. Inevitably, it also imbued them with strongly biblical views of man and society.

For the time being, the Remonstrant preachers continued their struggle in secret. However, already by 1630 their meetings were allowed as before. Many of the regents, especially in Holland, preferred the tolerant Remonstrants to the more fanatical Counter-Remonstrants, who disliked the power of civil government and would have preferred something of a theocracy. Tolerance, moreover, besides being morally preferable to many, also created a more open society which, especially to the merchants, also meant a society of commercial opportunities.

The execution of Johan van Oldenbarnevelt

Meanwhile Prince Maurice had taken high-handed action in several cities in Holland, replacing regents who sided with Oldenbarnevelt or the Remonstrants. The States-General condoned his actions and in 1618 even gave him full power; he then ordered the imprisonment of Oldenbarnevelt and his associates.

The subsequent trial of the Grand Pensionary, legally far from correct, was followed by his execution in May 1619. In a sense, this moment represented the culmination of the political and religious differences which had developed in the young Republic. At the age of 71, Oldenbarnevelt was convicted for his policies and for his efforts to have them observed. Actually, he was the victim of the wish of many, including, of course, Prince Maurice, that the power of the stadhouder and the States-General should prevail over the independence of the individual provinces, especially that of mighty Holland which threatened to dominate the others.

After the decapitation of Oldenbarnevelt, for some years Prince Maurice was the undisputed, although not formal ruler of the Republic. In 1620, he also became stadhouder of Groningen, which included the region of Drenthe. Consequently when the Twelve Years' Truce ended in 1621, he was able to once more continue war in the Spanish southern provinces, culminating in the relief of the besieged frontier town of Bergen op Zoom.

Anonymous portrait of Frederic–Henry of Nassau, prince of Orange (1584–1647)
RMA

On his death in 1625, Maurice was succeeded by another of William the Silent's sons, his half-brother Frederick Henry who became stadhouder in five of the seven provinces. Groningen now elected his cousin Ernst Casimir, who was already stadhouder in Friesland. Like Maurice, Frederick Henry continued to lead many successful campaigns against Spain. He conquered the towns of Den Bosch, Venlo, Roermond, Maastricht, Breda, Sas van Gent and Hulst for the Republic, which earned him the nickname 'Subduer of Cities'. Thus, part of the provinces of Brabant and Limburg, that had chosen to remain faithful to the Spanish king, now were forcefully added to the Republic's territory. Yet, the inhabitants remained Roman Catholics. This soon was to prove a problem, as people in the North felt these new citizens, adhering to the pope and, perhaps, to the king of Spain, could not really be trusted. Consequently, these two regions were not given full political rights within the Dutch Republic.

At sea, a decisive victory over the Spaniards was won in 1639, when admiral Maarten Tromp destroyed a second armada in English waters. Still, the northerners were unable to win an outright victory over the royal, southern Netherlands, but then again nor were the Spanish troops able to re-conquer the rebellious provinces.

15 1648: the Peace of Munster – the end of the Eighty Years' War

After a number of false starts, in 1640 negotiations were finally opened to arrange for another truce between Spain and the Republic. In Holland, and especially in Amsterdam, the leading politicians were beginning to realize that continuing the war would greatly harm trading interests; the other provinces, too, were war-weary, for the Republic had accumulated a gigantic debt, which pressed heavily on the population. Spain, too, was confronted with empty coffers. However, only in 1646 did all the seven provinces finally agree, with some even arguing for a definitive peace; in the meantime, the complexity of decision making in a confederation of seven almost autonomous republics had become patently obvious.

In 1646, a delegation of the States-General arrived at the German town of Munster, where representatives from France, Spain and the German Emperor had already gathered. Two more years of talks were needed on such complex issues as the international recognition of the sovereignty of the Netherlands and the freedom for Dutch merchants to trade with the Spanish East- and West-Indies - i.e. Asia and the Americas -, where they had infiltrated during the war and had successfully enlarged their commercial interests. Urged only half-heartedly by the Spaniards, who had been told to do so by the pope, freedom to worship for the Roman Catholics in the Republic was another demand during the peace talks. It was, however, not accepted. This meant that, for some two hundred years, almost half of the Dutch population had to worship in secret and, moreover, in other respects were treated as second-rate citizens as well.

The Munster-treaty was finally signed in 1648. Most important was the recognition by the Spanish king of the United Netherlands as a free and sovereign country. This sovereignty also was acknowledged by the Holy Roman Emperor who, since the ninth and tenth century, had been the nominal, but formally highest authority in the eastern provinces of the Northern Netherlands.

Another vital clause now excluded the Spaniards from trade with those areas in the East- and West-Indies that had been conquered by the Republic between 1598 and 1648. Essential to Dutch commercial interests was the decision that the River Scheldt was to remain closed to merchant shipping. This ensured the continued position of Amsterdam as the major international port of the Netherlands, because Antwerp was no longer able to compete. Obviously, this situation did little to endear the people of the North to their former 'brethren', especially in the Spanish states of Brabant and Flanders; though they might not have felt themselves to be part of one, 'Dutch' nation, they certainly shared a common language with the North, but now felt treated like enemies who were punished for remaining loyal to their lawful king and to the faith of their fathers.

Nevertheless, the Peace of Munster marked the end of the Eighty Years' War with Spain. It was the official seal on a situation that had arisen in 1579 when the rebellious provinces first had acceded to the Union of Utrecht.

The political structure of the Dutch Republic

It was mainly due to the efforts of Oldenbarnevelt that the now formally independent northern provinces had created a well-organized administration, albeit a complex one. Sovereignty lay with each of the seven provincial assemblies or States. Yet, according to the Union of Utrecht, their deputies in the States-General - the body that represented the confederation - were to decide on 'war and peace', in short on issues affecting foreign affairs; to complicate matters, decisions had to be unanimous. In each of the seven independent states, the by and large also independent cities carried great weight in the meetings of the provincial assemblies. The cities were governed by a 'vroedschap', a city council of 'wise' men who appointed civic officials. Recruited, mostly, from the urban elite, these councils co-opted new members when vacancies arose. This soon resulted in an oligarchic government: in most cities, a small number of regent families called the political and economic tune. In the rural areas of most provinces, power usually lay with the landowning families, most of whom were noble. Together with the urban representatives, they dominated the provincial States, since they appointing delegates from their midst to these periodical assemblies.

The seven provinces with the right to vote in the States-General were Holland, Zeeland, Utrecht, Friesland, Groningen, Overijssel and Gelderland, while Drenthe had a more limited degree of provincial sovereignty. A rather more different status was given to the 'Generality Lands', as the regions of Dutch Brabant, Flanders and Limburg now were called. They were governed not by independent provincial assemblies but directly by the States-General in which, however, they were not represented. This, of course, was the result

William II of Nassau, prince of Orange, aged 14, and his royal bride, Princess Mary Stuart of England, aged 9, depicted by Anthony van Dyck in 1641

Gerard ter Borch's famous painting of the ratification of the Peace of Munster in the Munster Town Hall on 15 May 1648
RMA

of their having been conquered from the Spanish government in Brussels during the campaigns of the decades between 1580 and 1640. In fact, they were considered, and, worse, treated as spoils of war. Another reason was that Catholicism had a strong following in these regions. No wonder that, for a very long time, many people there resented the enforced union with

the more northern provinces. Indeed, their feeling of being second-rate citizens, at most, and, moreover, of being economically and fiscally exploited
by their new masters did not foster a sense of Dutch nationhood amongst
them. In their turn, many Protestants feared that these 'Papist southerners' would eventually betray them.

16 The economy of the Golden Age: the Dutch Republic as the centre of world trade

From the 1580's onwards, Holland and Zeeland were economically flourishing; this was partly due to a stream of powerful or at least productive refugees from the southern Netherlands after the fall of Antwerp in 1585. Soon Amsterdam and Middelburg had taken over the role of Antwerp, previously the foremost trading centre of western Europe. Not surprisingly, Holland made sure to keep the Scheldt closed to shipping until well into the eighteenth century.

During the first decades of the seventeenth century, the two coastal states of the Republic became the centre of world trade, with Amsterdam as its hub. Several factors contributed to this situation. First, the success of the fishing industry and of international trade, both with their related forms of manufacture, which had started growing in the preceding centuries. Secondly, the absence of a protectionist economic policy, due to the absence of a truly central government that, as in most other European countries, would have been tempted to direct the economy. Such a policy would not have suited the seven autonomous little republics. Also, it was only natural that the leading merchants, who laid down the law in the government of Holland and Zeeland, conducted a foreign policy that promoted their own trade. Also, the Republic developed a well-functioning infrastructure as well as, at least in the cities, an educational system that resulted in one of the highest literacy rates in the world. Both factors obviously favoured economic growth. Last, but not least, the existence of large amounts of natural fuel, especially peat, provided a boost to the economy. However, in the five 'land provinces', the economy remained largely agricultural; in consequence, they did not enjoy the affluence the sea provinces acquired during the seventeenth century. This was reflected in the taxes levied to finance the joint policy of the seven republics: Holland alone paid 58% of the total dues.

The economic situation of the two major 'Generality Lands', Brabant and Limburg, that were largely rural, too, certainly deteriorated, if only because the States-General did not always act in their interest. One of the formerly prosperous cities that now lost its wealth because of this policy was 's Hertogenbosch, captured by Frederic Henry in 1629.

Trade to the Baltic, to the Straits of Gibraltar and to England

Already in the Middle Ages, the Netherlands had participated in trade with the Baltic. By the second half of the sixteenth century, Amsterdam was the European centre for the grain trade. This, in turn, led to the shipping of all kinds of other commodities. Salt, wine and spices from southern Europe, as well as herring and textiles were transported to the Baltic ports; Swedish copper was taken back on the return journey, to provide material for the arms industry. Dutch traders also sailed to Russia, buying large quantities of

fur and hides, as well as small but profitable quantities of caviar and gems. The Dutch merchant fleet was so active in trade with the Baltic that almost half of the ships that passed the tolls of the Danish Sound before 1650 were Dutch-owned. Holland and Zeeland rightly regarded trade to the Baltic as the 'mother' of their commercial wealth.

In addition, the so-called 'Straatvaart' or trade with southern Europe through the Straits of Gibraltar also flourished. Many of the commodities mentioned above were bought there, but the region also was important for Dutch exports, such as grain. After King Philip had closed the Spanish and Portuguese ports to Dutch trade in the 1580s and 1590s, merchant shipping branched out to find its way through the Straits to the Italian ports and especially the Levant. There, Asian products, which had been brought by overland caravans from Persia and India, were bought, to be sold again in western Europe.

Dutch traders also took an important part in the export of English products, such as wool and textiles, to the continent. On the other hand, they bought iron and coal in the river ports of central Europe, to be shipped to the North Sea by way of the Rhine and its Dutch tributaries.

A Dutch battleship cruising the Danish Sound, near Kronborg Castle, painted by Hendrik Vroom in 1614
RMA

p. 94-95
The return to Amsterdam of the second Dutch expedition to the East Indies, painted by Hendrik Vroom in 1599
RMA

Voyages of discovery, voyages of commerce

During the sixteenth century, the first century of Europe's large-scale contacts with the outside world, the Dutch had not taken part in voyages of discovery. Spain and Portugal had become the great colonial powers. Both countries were intent on finding new trade routes and on making as much profit as possible out of the conquered areas. For instance, America was important to Spain, both as the source of gold and silver, and as the region where large-scale, slave-worked plantations produced sugar, tobacco and, later, cotton. Meanwhile, Portugal had monopolized the trade in Asian spices.

When in 1580 Philip II of Spain captured Lisbon, the main gate through which spices passed into Europe, he closed its port to Dutch merchants who always came there to buy Asian products, though they had increasingly felt the Portuguese were unable to import as much as Europe needed. Consequently, the Dutch now seriously considered fetching spices themselves, and at the source: the Far East, an added advantage being that Portuguese distributors would no longer be able to push up the price. This decision was followed by Dutch expansion in the Americas, partly to wage economic war, there, on its enemy Spain, partly to participate in the trade opened between Africa and the Caribbean by the Portuguese and the Spaniards: a very lucrative trade, because it dealt in slaves.

Obviously, neither Spain nor Portugal was willing to let their competitors in on the secrets of the trade routes to Asia and the Americas. Therefore, the success of the Dutch ventures was mainly due to their thorough preparation and, one might add, their strong hope of profit. An important factor was the development of cartography, which reached an extremely high standard in the Netherlands at the end of the sixteenth century. The above-mentioned presence of many enterprising and wealthy merchants who had fled the Southern Netherlands also played a part: their previous experience in dealing with Spanish and Portuguese traders to Asia and their entrepreneurial fervour ensured that the Dutch expeditions were well equipped when they set out. Last but not least, the printed account of the travels of one John Huygen of Linschoten, who returned to the Netherlands in 1593 after spending thirteen years in Spain, Portugal and India, offered a wealth of important data, divulging a great deal of information the Portuguese would rather have kept to themselves.

The object of the first Dutch voyages to Asia certainly was not discovery as such, but finding a short, and therefore cheap North-East passage to Asia, i.e. along the Polar route. The most famous of these expeditions was the one led by Jacob van Heemskerck and Willem Barendsz., in 1596, instigated by Petrus Plancius, a Protestant minister but, more importantly, a skilled cartographer from Amsterdam; it was funded by a refugee from the South, the influential merchant Balthasar de Moucheron. The expedition stranded at Nova Zembla, where it was forced to spend the winter, but its discovery of the island of Spitsbergen was to be of some importance, as it became the centre of the Dutch whaling industry. Between 1595 and 1599, two expeditions set out to Southeast Asia by the traditional route, i.e. by

Title-page of Jan van Linschoten's travelogue of Asia (1596)

sailing around the Cape of Good Hope. The second of these, led by Jacob van Neck, was a great commercial success. Subsequently, a number of trading companies were established in several Dutch ports to promote regular trade with the East Indies, as the Far East was called.

Asian trading posts and commercial expansion: colonization?

Already during Van Neck's voyage, several factories, i.e. compact, defendable enclosures for storing goods and housing a few people - merchants and soldiers -, were set up in the Moluccas, the so-called Spice Islands situated in the eastern seas of Indonesia, to serve as bases for trade with the native population. These factories represented the earliest form of Dutch commercial expansion. Unlike the great colonial powers of the sixteenth century, Spain and Portugal, the Dutch did not envisage conquering lands to govern them and profit from them, or to use them as settlements for their own population. Indeed, their expansion long consisted of finding favourable locations for commerce, only. Gradually, however, some of these, mostly coastal, factories came to dominate the surrounding hinterland and its inhabitants. Yet, for the better part of the seventeenth and eighteenth centuries, the Dutch basically created an extensive and highly profitable trade network, rather than an empire. It only developed into a truly colonial venture in the course of the nineteenth century.

Hand-coloured title-page of the sixth volume of the 17th-century's most famous atlas, published by the Amsterdam firm of Joan Blaeu

The establishment of the United East India Company, or V.O.C.

The numerous small Dutch trading companies that were launched at the end of the sixteenth century competed so fiercely that the only way to ensure their continuing success lay in co-operation. Prince Maurice and Johan van Oldenbarnevelt, not yet the enemies they later became, worked together to unite them, aware of the political and economic importance of such an enterprise not only for Dutch commercial prosperity but, equally important, for enfeebling Spain and financing the war effort. Also, the establishment, in 1600, of the English East India Company was an incentive to concerted action.

In January 1602, representatives from the various companies met at The Hague at the invitation of the States-General, and decided upon the foundation of the (Dutch) United East India Company. Governed by a central committee, the so-called 'Gentlemen XVII', it was granted the monopoly of all Dutch trade to the Indies, or Asia, for a period of twenty-one years. This charter later was automatically prolonged, till the V.O.C.'s final failure at the very end of the eighteenth century.

Soon, the new company became a global organization, which has been called both the first joint-stock company of the world and the first multi-national in world economic history. Yet, though the exploits of the V.O.C. generally are considered among the most famous commercial activities of the Dutch, they never contributed more than 10% to the Republic's total trade volume. Admittedly, the dividends paid were sometimes extremely

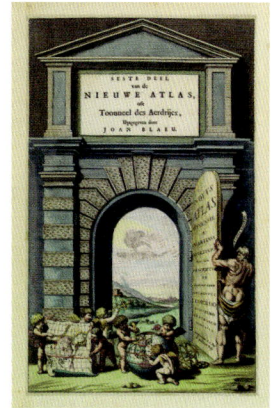

The castle of Batavia, the Asian headquarters of the Dutch EIC, seen from Kali Besar West, c. 1656, by A. Beeckman
RMA

high, and this, together with profitable speculation in Company shares, may well have accounted for its appeal amongst shareholders both at home and abroad. The Bourse in Amsterdam played an important part in transactions of this kind. It was built by Hendrick de Keyser between 1608 and 1611, in the architectural style of the London exchange. It soon was a, or even the centre of European trade in commodities and stock, V.O.C.-shares prominent among them. From the time of its opening, weekly price lists were printed and distributed all over Europe.

The Company was 'global', too, in the sense that it recruited its personnel - civic and military - from all over Europe. Actually, Germans and Scandinavians always formed a sizeable minority of its staff, both aboard its ships and in its Asian factories. However, it also employed a fair amount of men from the Asian countries it dealt with, mostly in a military capacity.

Junctions of a global trading network: the Cape Colony

In 1652, Jan van Riebeeck founded a settlement on the Cape of Good Hope, to serve the East-Indiamen as a staging post on their long journey to the Indies: a single trip from Amsterdam to the Dutch East-Indian capital at Batavia might well take three months. The Dutch were quick to settle at the Cape, soon also bringing Huguenots exiled from France. They mainly lived by farming and cattle breeding, thus provisioning the passing ships with fresh food. They also introduced viticulture which, thus,

formed the basis of South Africa's by now large share in the world's wine production. The native population, the nomadic Khoikhoi or Khoisan, called Hottentots by the Europeans, was forced to accept the influx of white immigrants. However, fierce struggles ensued with the African tribes who, coming from the north, during the seventeenth century also advanced on the Cape area.

During the nineteenth century, after the colony had been conquered by the British, many British as well as some German immigrants joined the European population in South Africa. From the very beginning, the Dutch and other European settlers were strongly opposed to interracial relations. But only during the nineteenth and early twentieth century did this result in a policy of increased forced segregation. This segregation, or 'Apartheid', turned into a symbol of persistent European racial imperialism when the non-Western world was freed from Western domination after the Second World War. It only was abolished in the last decade of the twentieth century.

Famously, the language of the 'Boers', the descendants of the Dutch farming population, is a vibrant branch of Dutch, producing its own high-quality literature even today.

The courtyard of the East India House in Amsterdam, c. 1875
RMA

Junctions of a global trading network: India and Sri Lanka

From the sixteenth century onwards, the south coasts of the Indian sub-continent had been dominated by the Portuguese, who monopolized the export of pepper to Europe. For the same reason, they attracted the Dutch, who managed to conquer most Portuguese factories during the seventeenth century. They established their centre at Cochin, on the Malabar Coast. They also invested in the indigenous pearl trade, and dealt extensively in textiles. In Bengal, where the Dutch were competing with other European agents, they established a very lucrative line in opium. However, they never managed to gain any ascendancy over India's vast interior.

The island of Ceylon, or Sri Lanka, the centre of cinnamon production, was a coveted possession as well. In the course of the seventeenth century, the Dutch ousted the Portuguese from their forts on the Ceylonese coasts, and forced the kings of Kandy, who ruled the interior, into cooperation. Such coastal cities as Colombo and Galle still show traces of Dutch rule, as do both the Ceylonese language, which adopted a number of Dutch words and, more surprisingly, the legal system, which is a fascinating combination of so-called Dutch-Roman law and other European and indigenous elements.

The third governor-general of the Dutch East Indies, Jan Pieterszoon Coen (1587–1629)

Junctions of a global trading network: Java and the Spice Islands

The first Dutch contacts with Asia had aimed at the trade in cloves and mace, which were mainly produced on a few islands in the east of the Indonesian archipelago. As the Portuguese had settled there, first, the Dutch were faced with the necessity to unsettle them, which they did successfully, albeit with some force. However, since the Dutch, like the other Europeans, lacked the bullion to engage in large-scale intra-Asian trade, and, moreover, had to find some means to feed their factories in the Indies, they soon turned to the main island of Java as well; it not only produced great quantities of rice, but also was the place where, at Bantam, the trade of Southeast Asia had one of its traditional centres.

Finally, in 1619 the Dutch conquered the small state of Jakatra and built a fort, there, where they concentrated the administration of their operations in the entire Asian region. In the town which grew around the fort, and which they called Batavia - the present Djakarta -, the governor-general of the Dutch East Indies resided. To him, and to his 'Council of the Indies', did the many dozens of factories all around the Indian Ocean annually report. Batavia also was the major destination of the annual fleets that arrived from the Republic, bringing orders from the Gentlemen XVII, bringing new merchants, bringing soldiers, bringing Protestant ministers, et cetera. From Batavia, a fleet set out again on its homebound journey, laden with costly Asian wares.

The interior of Java, till the beginning of the eighteenth century, largely remained in the hands of native rulers. These, however, increasingly sought the Company's support in their mutual wars. To ensure food supplies and protect its other commercial interests, the V.O.C. was drawn into, and started mingling in, the politics of the interior. Thus, by the end of the century the Company not only ruled the coasts of Java, it also had begun to advance upon the inland principalities.

Junctions of a global trading network: China and Japan

To all Europeans, the 'Middle Empire', China, was a major commercial goal, offering the possibility to trade in the very profitable 'china ware': porcelain and silk and, later, tea. While they all sought to gain access to the production centres of these luxury commodities, the Chinese authorities managed to keep the foreigners out. Though the Dutch tried to infiltrate mainland China, they did not succeed, either. But they did occupy the island of Taiwan, or Formosa, formerly held by the Portuguese, which allowed them to keep up a lucrative smuggling trade with the continent. In the eighteenth century, the Dutch also kept a factory at the great commercial port of Canton, recently opened to foreigners, where they traded in tea and other products.

The Dutch were far more successful in Japan. Already in 1600, the first Dutch ship, 'De Liefde', entered a Japanese port. Soon, a lively trade resulted, which gave the Dutch copper, lacquer work, silk and porcelain. When, due to internal political developments, the Japanese government decided to oust all foreigners, especially the V.O.C's main rivals Portugal and England, the Dutch were the only ones they allowed to stay on. Though the Dutch were virtually imprisoned on the tiny island of Deshima, in the Bay of Nagasaki, they were given permission to send a trading ship to Japan each year. Also annually, the Dutch were forced to travel to the shogun capital, Edo, present-day Tokyo, to negotiate the prolongation of the trading concessions. Soon, a situation grew in which the Japanese used the Dutch to learn about European customs and culture, especially the sciences, while the servants of the V.O.C. became Europe's main informants about the culture and institutions of Japan, especially through the travelogues they published.

The Americas: piracy and the establishment of the Dutch West India Company, or W.I.C.

In addition to Asian trade via the Cape and the Indian Ocean, at the beginning of the seventeenth century Dutch merchant shipping also made its way westward. In 1609, Henry Hudson, while looking for a northern passage to the Indies for the V.O.C., discovered the bay in North America that is named after him. But the westward voyages across the Atlantic Ocean had a different goal, namely piracy. This was a weapon in the ongoing war against Spain, aiming to hit the enemy state in its financial heart, the annual fleet leaving the Americas with gold and silver. If it arrived safely in Seville, its treasures helped to finance Spanish military operations in Europe and Asia.

However, Oldenbarnevelt did not favour founding a West India Company for this specific purpose. His objections were not principled, though, since piracy was common practice all over Europe. Rather, this veiled way of funding piracy conflicted with his desire for peace with Spain. However, his adversary, Prince Maurice, did not share these scruples as it suited him to be at war. Hence, he supported the project for a Dutch W.I.C. In 1621, soon after Oldenbarnevelt's execution, it was finally established. However, trade eventually became the main object of this company, too, particularly the slave trade from Africa to the Americas, providing the labour force for the plantations founded by the European settlers. Yet, as Oldenbarnevelt had feared, privateering prevailed for a long time. The greatest prize won by the Dutch was the capture, by Admiral Piet Hein, in 1628, of the Spanish silver fleet. The event still is remembered in one of the most popular Dutch folk songs.

Junctions of a global trading network: 'Holland on the Hudson' and the Brazilian failure.

Unlike in Asia, the Dutch did actually engage in colonization in the Americas, specifically in the Windward Islands (even now an integral part of the Kingdom of the Netherlands), and in Brazil. The latter was highly important because it catered to Europe's growing need of such delicacies

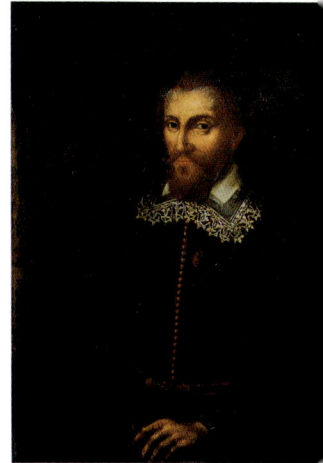

Pieter Both (1550–1615), first governor-general of the Dutch East Indies (1609–1614)
RMA

One of the most famous admirals of the Dutch fleet, Piet Hein (1577–1629), who became a national hero when, in 1628, he captured the Spanish treasure fleet in the Caribbean

as tobacco and sugar, as well as in 'brazil wood'. For some twenty years, the Dutch held the north-eastern part of this region, around the town of Recife which they captured from the Portuguese. In the end, however, they had to relinquish their colony again. Meanwhile, the 'Mauritshuis' at The Hague, today one of the later foremost museums, was built with Brazilian gold amassed by the last Dutch governor of the colony, Prince Maurice of Nasau-Siegen, who also had the peoples of his colony described and depicted by a number of Dutch scholars and artists, thus creating a valuable source of knowledge of cultures that did not describe and depict themselves.

From the late sixteenth century onwards, North America, which had not been colonized by the Spanish or the Portuguese, lay open to other European conquerors, who hoped to find there the same riches the Iberians had found in Central and South-America. At the mouth of the Hudson, the Dutch established a colony-cum-trading post, which they used as a base from which to contact the Indian tribes who lived along the river and provided them with furs and hides. From 1629 onwards, a number of Dutch families moved inland, creating several sometimes very extensive estates, or 'patroonships'. A number of names of cities and villages bear witness to this episode as does, of course, some of the Dutch-style architecture. Even the metropolis now known as New York was first founded by the Dutch on Manhattan Island, and aptly named New Amsterdam. It had its "wall", hence 'wall-street', and, nearby, another village called "Breukelen", hence 'Brooklyn', et cetera. In 1667, however, the English forced the Dutch to cede this colony as part of a peace settlement following a war they had won.

Actually, the West India Company never fully exploited the trading and other potential of this settlement, partly due to lack of vision, partly due to lack of capital. Indeed, the Company never achieved the stature of its East India counterpart.

Junctions of a global trading network: Surinam

When the English claimed New Amsterdam to round off their North-American colonies, the Dutch were not entirely unwilling to accept Surinam, on the Northeast coast of South America, in compensation. The region was thought to provide an entry into the (largely imaginary) gold reserves of the interior. Though by that time the first W.I.C. had gone bankrupt, it was re-established in the 1670's, now to govern and exploit Suri-

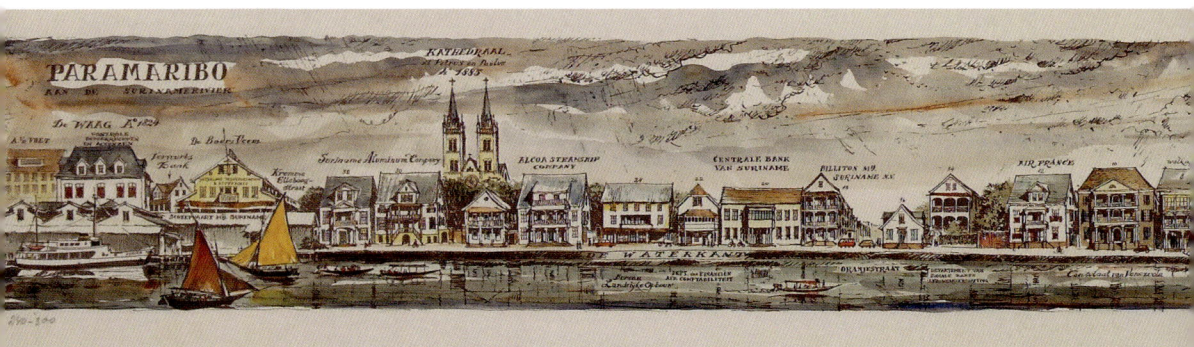

nam, which was settled by Dutchmen, by Protestant Huguenots escaping royal and Roman Catholic intolerance in France, and by Jewish refugees who had fled religious and economic persecution on the Iberian peninsula. Mostly, they founded plantations there, to produce sugar and other products for the European market. To cultivate the land, the Company imported numerous slaves from West Africa. To ensure a steady supply, the Dutch joined other European countries, such as Portugal and England, in the acquisition of slaves sold to them by native African traders. To deal with the traders from the African interior, the Dutch captured a number of forts established on the west or 'Slave' coast of Africa by the Portuguese.

The rise of industry

In the seventeenth century, the flourishing of Dutch international trade encouraged the rise of various industries. Shipbuilding boomed in the Zaan-region and supply companies such as ropeyards and sail makers profited as well. Trade also promoted a number of processing industries, that worked with imported raw materials or semi-finished products, as in sugar refining.

In addition to these trade-related industries, other sectors of the economy prospered as well, as a result of the rapidly growing markets and, again, the arrival of refugees from the South, many of them skilled workers. Soon, the production of cloth in the textile industry at Leiden reached great heights, stimulated by skilled Flemish weavers who introduced new techniques.

Inevitably, the fame of this prospering industry attracted labourers from the far less prosperous German rural regions that bordered on the Dutch Republic. Generally speaking, of course, labour and its price determined the ability of Dutch industry to compete on the European market. With growing taxes and the cost of labour rising as well, this very ability declined during the later decades of the seventeenth century.

It is important to realize that Holland and Zeeland benefitted most from the prosperity that trade and industry brought, as did Friesland, to a lesser degree. In the other provinces, agriculture remained the main source of income. There, trade and manufacture maintained the same low level as in previous centuries, which inevitably resulted in the contrast with the prosperous coastal provinces becoming steadily more marked.

European urbanism in the tropics: the waterfront of Paramaribo, capital of the Dutch colony of Surinam
Atlas van Stolk

The grand-scale reclamation of land

The continuing and even increased reclamation of land in the northern region of Holland was a direct result of the prosperity ensuing from trade and industry. It now became essential to enlarge the cultivated area, if only to ensure that the growing

population did not become totally dependent on food imports, but, if possible, even would produce a surplus for export as well. During the seventeenth century, many leading citizens invested their money in the reclamation business, like the famous poet and senior civil servant Jacob Cats, as well as such capitalists as Dirck van Os, an executive of the V.O.C.

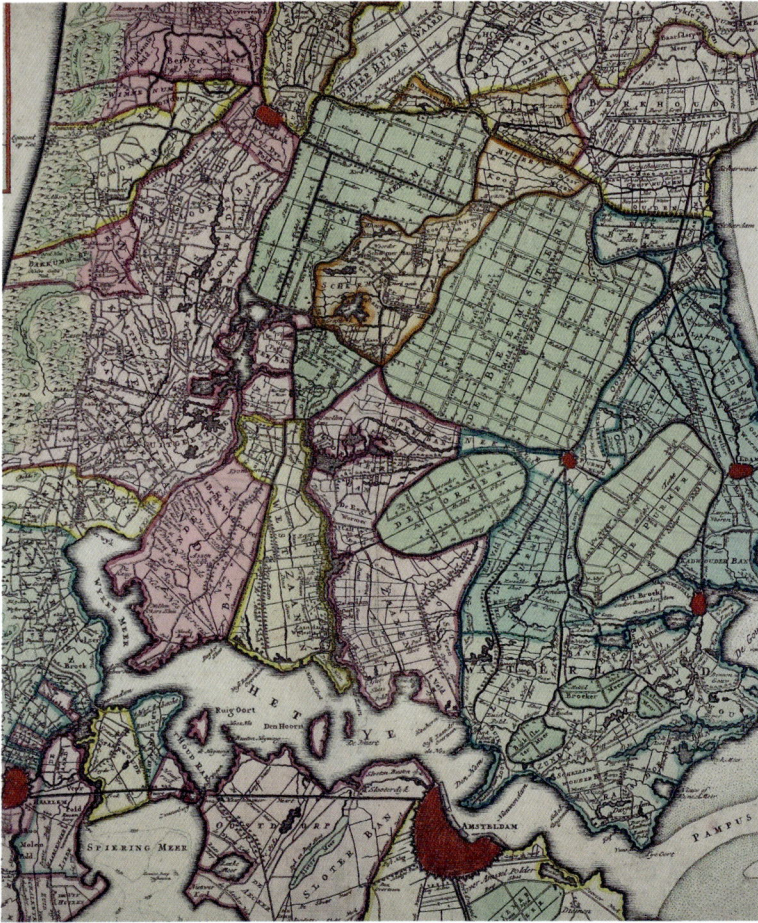

Map of the Beemsterpolder, showing the grid of ditches dug in 1610 to reclaim some 72 square kilometres of arable land

The Beemster, one of the county's largest lakes, was drained between 1608 and 1610 on the basis of techniques developed by Jan Adriaansz. Leeghwater and the energy provided by fifty windmills. In the course of the next twenty-five years, some 37.000 acres of land were reclaimed for farming by also draining other watery parts of North Holland into 'polders'.

Stagnation or decline?

The period during which the Republic dominated European and, to some extent, global trade reached its zenith between 1630 and 1650. At that time, the Dutch merchant fleet consisted of over 2500 ships, with at least another 2000 fishing vessels, mostly herring 'busses'. A very gradual decline set in after 1650, not yet really affecting the prosperity of the Republic but slowly eroding its undisputed leading role in Europe's world economy. Yet, in the mean time, the prosperity of the western provinces of the Northern Netherlands had resulted in a blossoming of the arts and sciences as never before.

17   The civilisation of the Dutch Golden Age

The Dutch Republic as a 'burgher state'

The Dutch Republic was a polity and a society unlike most other European states in that it was ruled and governed not by a monarch and an attendant nobility and clergy, but by a bourgeois elite. The influence of the ensuing burgher culture was particularly strong in the various arts. From the late fifteenth and early sixteenth century onwards, the prosperous burghers had first competed with the nobility and clergy in commissioning works of art, mainly collectively, and usually in architecture and (religious) painting. By the seventeenth century, the role played by nobles and clergy in the patronage of the arts was almost entirely taken over by the burgher elite.

Painting: genre pictures, portraits and other

Bourgeois patronage first and foremost became visible in painting. Even today people are amazed at the enormous quantity of high-quality paintings produced in the Dutch Republic, covering nearly all genres, though precisely religious art declined, understandably, of course, in what was, increasingly, a Protestant society. In the seventeenth century, foreign visitors often were surprised when confronted with the huge amounts of paintings offered for sale on ordinary weekday markets and fairs. They also were astonished to note that even simple artisans and farmers actually bought and owned such works.

Inevitably, this situation had a definite impact on the painting 'industry', with painters now specializing in sometimes very narrow fields, as well as on the choice of topics. In seventeenth-century Holland, a unique style emerged, specifically in the many genre pictures that were produced to satisfy the taste of the general public. The treatment of the subjects usually was moralistic, in the spirit of the writer Jacob Cats, whose literary work was very popular if only because he exhibited a judicious combination of business acumen and soberness with the pleasure of life that greatly appealed to the pious, yet art-loving middle classes.

Portraits were almost equally popular: portraits of individual burghers - men, women and also children - but even more striking group portraits, depicting the sedately-looking men and women who constituted the numerous boards of governors of commercial companies and civic and

Frederic–Henry of Nassau, prince of Orange, with his wife, Amalia of Solms, and their three daughters, by Gerard van Honthorst (1647)
RMA

charitable institutions. These paintings expressed both their pride in their position, and, of course, their status in society. Famous amongst the many painters who produced these group portraits were Bartholomeus van der Helst (1613-1670) and Frans Hals (1580-1666). By far the best-known picture in this context is, of course, the one commissioned by the members of the Amsterdam militia-company of Captain Frans Banning Cock. Painted in 1642, by Rembrandt van Rijn (1606-1669), it was not a success at all. Only during the romantic nineteenth century, when it became known as 'The Night Watch', it was hailed as the most perfect example of Dutch Golden Age-art.

Also much sought after were landscapes and, of course, marines or seascapes, often revealing the pride the Dutch took in their naval exploits. Still lives were popular, too, both those which showed sumptuously decked tables laden with heaps of costly food and simple scenes of a few fruits, vegetables or other foodstuffs. Actually, both this abundance and the sobriety were, actually, meant as a warning against excess.

Baroque (religious) art

While all these pictures catered to the taste of the wealthier burghers, the aristocracy, and the Catholics, now worshipping in private, demanded a different approach. Painting produced for them was more ambitious in content and more sophisticated, reflecting a cosmopolitan culture, relating strongly to the international Baroque style that had developed in Italy.

In the sixteenth and early seventeenth century, artists working in this fashion usually belonged to the 'School of Utrecht', not surprisingly since this cathedral city remained staunchly Catholic even after the Reformation. Dutch Baroque painting received a new impetus when a number of artists from Antwerp settled in Haarlem. They worked in the late-Baroque style, called Mannerism. Often, this kind of work, mainly depicting biblical scenes, was commissioned by wealthy Catholics to adorn their 'secret' churches. The earliest representative of this group was Karel van Mander (1548-1606), also known for his 'Book of Artists', containing the biographies of some of the most famous Dutch painters of the time. Hendrick Goltzius (1558-1617), a skilled engraver who specialized in coloured woodprints, was instrumental in spreading this kind of art amongst a wider public.

Paintings by artists of the Utrecht School also were in demand at the internationally orientated court of Prince Frederick Henry. After his death in 1647, his widow, Amalia van Solms, decided to have the central, domed hall of the newly-built Range-residence, 'Huis ten Bosch', on the outskirts of The Hague, adorned with a series of murals and ceiling paintings in the grand manner, the work of some thirteen painters. Specifically the so-called 'Orange Hall' of this summer palace, where the present king resides, shows elaborate scenes from the life of her late husband, to glorify the Orange family. Rembrandt, too, painted for the court, in this Baroque manner. He also was one of the few artists outside the Utrecht School to paint religious pictures as well: from his earliest days as a pupil, the Bible had been a major source of inspiration.

While this is not the place to outline the variety of seventeenth-century Dutch painting in any more detail, Gerard Ter Borch (1617-1681) is an artist deserving special mention, not because his work was in any way more remarkable than that of most of his fellow-artists, but because, of his own accord, he immortalized one of the most momentous events in the history of the early Republic: he was the one who depicted the Dutch and foreign diplomats in the act of ratifying the epochal Treaty of Munster, in 1648.

Architecture and interior decoration: the Renaissance, 'Dutch Classicism' and the Baroque

Admittedly, during the second half of the sixteenth century Renaissance elements began to cover buildings that still were Gothic in structure; as yet, the ideal of Italian Renaissance architecture, the quest for perfect spatial dimensions in the right proportions, had not been taken up in the North. In the seventeenth century, burghers took a more active part in commissioning buildings, both for their private use and for civic, collective purposes,

The famous Stock
Exchange of
Amsterdam, built by
Hendrick de Keyser
between 1608 and 1611
GAA

A vase to hold tulips,
in the Delftware
that tried to emulate
Chinese Ming por-
celain

and demanded the more fashionable style introduced from Italy.

Wealthy Amsterdam set the tone. Due to the rapidly increasing population, a substantial enlargement of the city became necessary. By the year 1600, Hendrick de Keyser (1565-1621) was the leading Dutch architect. No wonder he was asked to build many of the dwellings that were constructed along the new canals that, in three concentric rings (called the Herengracht, the Keizersgracht and the Prinsengracht) gave the city its even now characteristic image. Some of the often palatial houses designed by him and others show Renaissance characteristics, some, including the famous 'Trippenhuis', the work of the architect Jacob Vingboons for the eponymous family of enormously rich entrepreneurs and traders, are in a majestic classical style. All reflect the wealth and good taste of the merchant-regents, not only of Amsterdam and of the other Holland towns but also of Zeeland, Utrecht, Groningen and Friesland, where one finds examples only slightly less sumptuous.

Collectively, these men also commissioned a variety of civic buildings as well as churches. While the Zuiderkerk and the Westerkerk in Amsterdam rank amongst the best examples of the mixed Gothic-classical style in Dutch church architecture, surely one of the most beautiful achievements in seventeenth-century civic architecture is the Amsterdam Town Hall, now the royal palace, on the Dam Square.It was designed by Jacob van Campen (1595-1657) and shows many typically Dutch characteristics, since the architect worked in a restrained classical style that has been called Dutch Classicism. Still, with its sculptures and paintings that, together, form a grand, allegorical scheme presenting Amsterdam in all its glory as the centre of world trade - visualized in the huge marble maps of the world embedded in the floor of the building's main hall - it came to embody the ideal of the Baroque: an integral work of art.

With its colonial connections, Dutch society knew of Asia's magnificent material culture. Lacquer work from Japan was very popular, but Chinese and Japanese porcelain was an even more status-enhancing possession. However, Dutch efforts to reproduce the precious 'china' failed. Yet, in the process, the ceramics industry, especially at Delft, did succeed in producing beautiful stoneware itself that soon became almost equally desirable: 'Delftware' has been a brand name ever since. All this oriental luxury mixed and matched with furniture mostly in the Baroque style.

In these years, gardens became an extension of architecture, being laid out in formal geometric patterns, with flower beds filled with single coloured flowers, including, of course, the hugely popular tulip, seen as specifically Dutch, though it came from Turkey. When William III of Orange moved to England in 1688, Dutch culture, both in architecture and in gardening, moved with him, influencing elite culture, there. For a few decades, other countries such as Sweden and Brandenburg-Prussia looked to Holland, too, for inspiration in these specific fields.

Literature: the Muiden Circle

In literature, too, a specifically Dutch style of writing that already had evolved during the sixteenth century now was maturing. One of the qualities for which the Dutch were known in the following centuries was tolerance towards dissidents, this despite the fact that mercenary arguments definitely played their part as well. This tolerance was illustrated in the literary work of Dirk Coornhert (1522-1590), a follower of Erasmus. The 'Eglantine Chamber of Rhetoric', at Amsterdam, did much to stimulate both poetry and playwriting reflecting these ethical ideas. Such literary lights as Hendrik Spiegel (1549-1612) and Pieter Roemer Visscher (1547-1620) were among its members. Their work is characterized by a moralizing view of the world that was echoed in seventeenth-century painting.

The Amsterdam home of the merchant and poet Visscher was the venue for a large circle of painters, writers and musicians, who included his gifted daughters Anna and Maria Tesselschade. After his death, these gatherings relocated to Muiden Castle, the seat of another great author, Pieter Corneliszn Hooft (1581-1647). Though in no way a formal institution, between 1610 and 1647, it was a hub of cultural and scientific activity. The variety of religious and political backgrounds represented in the so-called Muider Circle reflected the relatively tolerant social climate of the Dutch upper class during the seventeenth century. The fierce disputes between Remonstrants and Counter-Remonstrants had cast a shadow, but no lasting damage had been done.

Significantly, Hooft, the man who played host to the Muiden Circle, was a burgomaster's son from Amsterdam who had been appointed bailiff of Muiden by Prince Maurice in 1609. He wrote a number of plays, including a comedy called *Ware-nar*, an adaptation of a piece by the Roman writer Plautus. Hooft's style was characteristic of the development of literature in the Netherlands. Towards the end of the sixteenth century, writers had been trying to find their own ways of expressing themselves. Now, authors increasingly found inspiration in ancient Greek and Roman authors. As a historiographer, too, Hooft turned to ancient Rome for inspiration, when he started writing his great history of the early Dutch republic: Tacitus's 'Annals' served as a model for his 'Histories'.

The poet and statesman Jacob Cats (1577–1660), by Michiel van Mierevelt (1639)
RMA

The writer Pieter Corneliszoon Hooft (1581–1647), by Michiel van Mierevelt (1629)
RMA

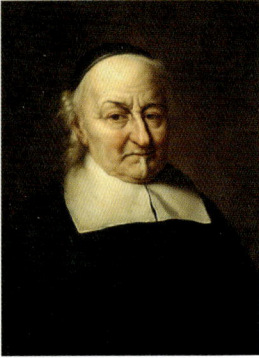

The 'prince' of the
Dutch poets, Joost van
den Vondel (1587–1679)
RMA

Joost van den Vondel: the 'prince of poets'

Another text in the classical vein was the tragedy *Palamedes*, though it had a plot based on a contemporary event, the judicial murder of Oldenbarnevelt. Its author, Joost van den Vondel (1587-1679), a Roman Catholic, also was a regular visitor of Muiden Castle. Considered by many the greatest Dutch poet of the century, he risked his life with this work that was published in 1625. When the Amsterdam burgomasters, proud of the genius who gave fame to their town, let him off with a moderate fine, he wrote another politically-laden tragedy, in defence of the Catholic Mary Stuart, Queen of Scots who had been beheaded by her Protestant rival Elisabeth. A comedy by Vondel, *Leeuwendalers*, was performed with great success at the Amsterdam Theatre to celebrate the Peace of Munster.

Vondel's tragedy *Gijsbrecht van Aemstel* provided the people of Amsterdam with an inspiring though historically inaccurate, for rather more allegorical version of an early episode of their town's history, stressing its historic independence from the counts of Holland and, thus, from contemporary efforts by the States of Holland to dominate this mighty town. Indicative of the true cosmopolitanism of a number of artists working in seventeenth-century Amsterdam is the fact that Vondel was among the very first European writers to base a literary text, and a play at that, on a non-European event: his tragedy *Zungchin* was set against the background of the recent, dramatic change of power in imperial China. However, Vondel's most important plays undoubtedly are his biblical tragedies, of which *Lucifer* surely ranks among the greatest written in seventeenth-century Europe.

The scholar and lawyer
Hugo de Groot (1583–1645)
RMA

Hugo de Groot: founder of international law

Another visitor of the literary and musical gatherings at Muiden Castle was Hugo de Groot (1583-1645) or 'Grotius', playwright, mathematician, theologian, historian and, last but not least, legal scholar. He had been one of the political leaders of the Remonstrants, for which reason he was imprisoned in Loevestein Castle in 1619. He reputedly made a spectacular escape in a book chest, after which he was forced to live in exile. His *De Jure Belli ac Pacis libri tres*, 'Three Books on War and Peace', which appeared in 1625, laid the foundation for international law. In other writings, he defended the freedom of the seas, and of international trade, hardly surprisingly in view of the fact that he used to be the head of the Dutch East India Company's legal department and thus wrote to please his masters. Like so many of his contemporaries, he strongly believed in religious freedom, advocating tolerance in a number of his shorter writings.

Music

There was music too, in Hooft's Muiden-group. Maria Tesselschade Visscher often was accompanied by the Portuguese-Jewish vocalist Francisca Duarte, who would sing compositions set to the poems of the statesman-poet-composer Constantijn Huygens, who was one of the century's most accomplished lyricists and himself a member of the group. Jan Pieterszoon Sweelinck (1562-1621), employed at the Old Church at Amsterdam, was a welcome guest as well. One of the greatest organ players and composers of his day, he had many German pupils. He invented the genre of the fugue that, a century later, was developed to perfection by Johan Sebastian Bach. He also wrote some impressively beautiful vocal music, mostly as a setting of the biblical psalms.

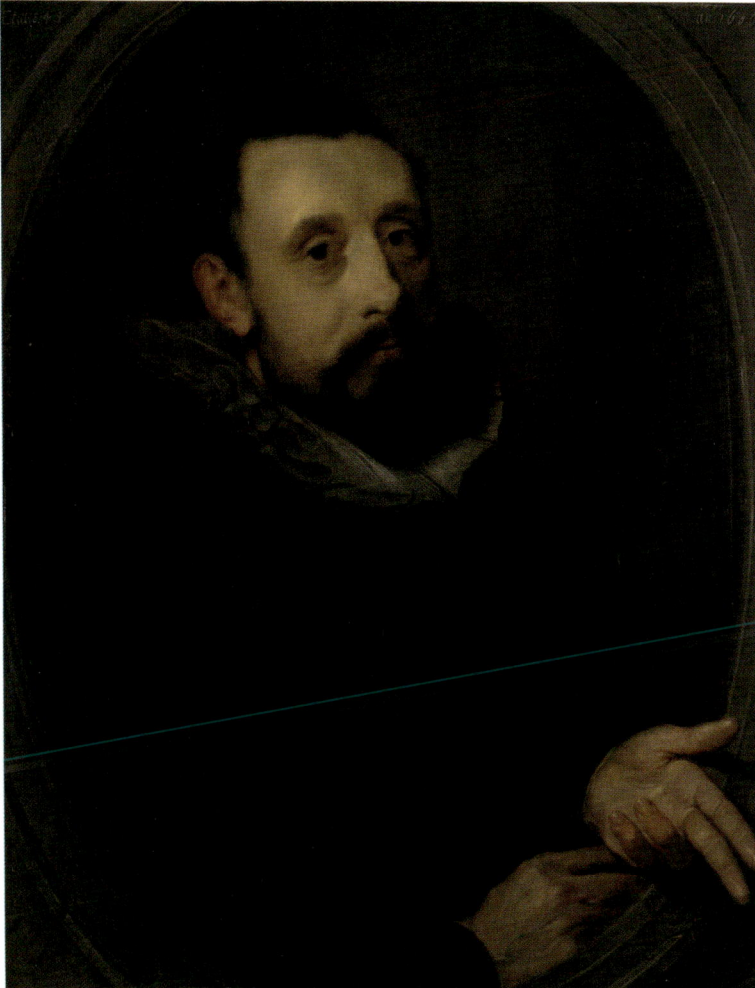

The composer Jan Pieterszoon Sweelinck (1562–1621)

The medical scientist Herman Boerhave (1668–1738), whose textbooks on medicine and chemistry were used all over Europe and, even, in China and Japan

Science and education

The transition to Protestantism as the privileged religion of the state had far-reaching effects on Dutch education. The first university in the north, at Leiden, was founded with the precise object of providing adequate training facilities for Protestant, or as they soon were called 'Dutch-Reformed' ministers. Other towns were eager to establish their own institutions of higher education in the wake of Leiden University, not only to show civic pride but also to provide schooling for the elite of regents and wealthy merchants, beyond the level taught at the traditional Latin schools. One such college was founded in Franeker in 1585, another in Utrecht in 1636 and yet another in Harderwijk in 1645. Nijmegen, too, had its own, though short-lived university, for as these institutions were paid for by the cities, rather than by a wealthy, centralised state, they did precariously depend on a town's financial situation. One of the men who joined the many writers, musicians and scholars at Muiden Castle was Gerardus Johannes Voss, whose name was commonly Latinized as Vossius. He was a professor of history at the 'Athenaeum Illustre', a college of higher education founded in Amsterdam in 1632 with standards equalling those of Leiden University. Leiden itself attracted many scholars, such as the Oriental scholar Jacob Golius, and the Classicist and poet Daniel Heinsius. Their learned fame induced students from all over Europe to come to Holland.

In secondary education, too, changes occurred. During the seventeenth century, schools for middle-class children were founded with the specific aim to provide a less bookish, academic-orientated, more practical, commercial education. These were the 'French' schools, where the subjects taught were French, geography and arithmetic, besides, of course, in true Calvinist tradition, religion and ethics. Most of the French schools were run privately, with boarding facilities for the mostly male pupils.

Of course, since the Reformation, knowledge of Latin, that had been and remained one of the mainstays of the curriculum of the Latin schools, was no longer the language of the Church, as services were now conducted in Dutch. Moreover, as it was essential for the propagation of Calvinism that as many people as possible could read the Bible, this was translated and printed in the vernacular, too. In view of this new situation, so-called 'Dutch Schools' were founded everywhere, usually at the instigation of church- or town councils. They only taught the most elementary subjects such as reading and writing. Even arithmetic was not part of the standard curriculum, though it seems that in the more commercially orientated parts of the country this was soon introduced. Meanwhile, as indicated above all this educational activity did ensure that the rate of literacy in the Dutch Republic remained among the highest in the contemporary world.

However, these universities and other educational institutions were no hotbeds of scientific research, certainly not of the sort of 'big', laboratory-based science that has come to dominate present-day society. Indeed, experimental science was by and large an activity pursued by individuals or by small groups of like-minded, usually wealthy persons who, rather than being professional scientists, mostly were amateurs. Anthonie van Leeuwenhoek, the first to discover and describe microbes, originally was a merchant, who, in his free time, created the lenses for a self-constructed microscope that allowed him to do his important work in cell-biology. Cornelis Drebbel, who built one of the first operational submarines, worked all by himself as well. Last, but not least, Christiaan Huygens, son of the famous poet-statesman, was a major figure in the international debate on astronomy, as well as an inventor of, amongst other things, the pendulum clock. Quietly working at home, he had no university affiliation what so ever.

Science and scholarship in the Dutch Republic also were influenced by foreigners, since many intellectuals, escaping persecution in their home countries, settled there because of the tolerant religious climate. Thus, Pierre Bayle, one of the forerunners of Enlightenment culture, spent most of his life in Rotterdam, publishing his hugely influential 'Dictionary', really an encyclopaedia as well as a text arguing the need for empirical, objective research free of preconceived religious notions.

In this vibrant cultural climate, where, moreover, new books were being published every year to an extent not equalled elsewhere, many people who lacked the money and the time to buy and read longish texts felt the need for short, authoritative introductions to newly-gained knowledge. Thus, in the 1690's, one Pieter Rabus produced the first periodical catering to this kind of readership, a sort of early *Reader's Digest*.

Anthonie van Leeuwenhoek (1632–1723), self-made scholar but yet world-famous scientist in the field of microbiology

18 Society and politics in the second half of the seventeenth century

Stadhouder William II

After the Peace of Munster, England, though a Protestant nation, too, soon became one of the most powerful enemies of the Dutch Republic. Of course, trade rivalry had been endemic between the two regions since the Middle Ages, but now increased as the Republic started on a more structured policy of economic expansion. Another reason for the conflict that now ensued was that William II of Orange, Frederic Henry's only son and heir, supported the cause of the English Stuarts who had been banished by the revolutionary leader Oliver Cromwell after the execution of King Charles I in 1649. William's stance was not surprising: he was married to the late king's daughter Mary. However, both for commercial and ideological reasons, most of the city regents were opposed to the stubborn stadhouder's wish to intervene on behalf of the English royals.

Indeed, the relationship of the urban elite of Holland with the House of Orange had cooled already after the Peace of Munster had been agreed upon against William's will. It did not improve when, in 1650, the States of Holland announced that they would no longer shoulder the expense of the 42 regiments that constituted their part of the country's costly militia. William then caused a resolution to be passed by the States-General, ordering the army captains to remain in charge of their companies. Bringing along troops, he then embarked on a rather unfriendly visit of those cities of Holland that had the right to vote in the provincial States. The opposition he met wherever he went led him to imprison six leading regents in Loevestein Castle. Rebellious Amsterdam was even threatened by an army under William Frederick, stadhouder of Friesland. Finally, the city agreed to support the Prince in the States of Holland.

Anonymous portrait of William II of Nassau, prince of Orange (1626–1650)
RMA

Prins Wilhelm van Orangien

Ætatis 25 obijt in den Haagh, 1650

The First Stadhouderless Period 1650–1672

However, much to the relief of many, William died suddenly at the end of 1650. There was no immediate heir as his only son was born nine days after his father's death. This confronted the young Republic with a new situation. A 'Grand Assembly' was convened at The Hague to deliberate on future policy. To it, each of the provinces sent a large group of representatives. The issues were 'unity, the army and religion', with each of the seven provinces stressing the need that their full sovereignty on each issue be respected. To ensure their own power and independence, they decided not to appoint a new stadhouder for the time being.

The Navigation Act: the first 'English', or Anglo-Dutch war

Meanwhile, the continuing economic success of the Republic since the 1580's had increased jealousy abroad, specifically in England. There, in 1651 a Navigation Act was passed for the protection of English shipping and trade. It decreed that European goods were only to be imported into England by English ships or by ships from the country of origin, thus robbing the Dutch merchant fleet of one of its major sources of income. Also, coastal trade with England was out of bounds to foreign shipping from then on.

This English intervention in the international free-trade system zealously promoted by the Republic and aimed at one of the main elements in Dutch commercial success, the freight trade, resulted in the first Anglo-Dutch war (1652-1654). It was a bad war for the Republic. After a 'Three-Days' Battle' at sea, the English ruled the waves, even blockading the coast of Holland.

During the peace negotiations, representatives of the by now Lord Protector Cromwell demanded guarantees from the Republic that the House of Orange would never be reinstated in its position of power, showing his fear that the family would support the restoration of a Stuart monarchy. The States-General and the States of Holland again held opposing views on this point and this time Holland came off best.

A few weeks after the Peace of Westminster had been signed in 1654, Holland decided that no prince of Orange would ever be appointed stadhouder or admiral of the province again. They would also oppose the appointment of an Orange to the position of captain-general of the union by the States-General. This was known as the 'Act of Seclusion'; secretly, it had already been included in the peace treaty with England.

The plan had been devised by the grand pensionary of Holland, Johan de Witt (1625-1672). Hailing from the powerful commercial town of Dordrecht, he had been in charge of the politics of Holland since 1653. Originally, his ideas on this and other points met with opposition from the other provinces, but his marriage to the daughter of one of Amsterdam's leading regents brought this influential city into his camp, strengthening his position.

CONCORDIA RES PARVE

The Knights' Hall of the former palace of the counts of Holland at The Hague, used by the States-General for its famous 'Grand Assembly' in 1651
RMA

Portrait of William III
of Nassau (1650–1702),
prince of Orange as
well as, from 1689 till
1702, king of Great
Britain and Ireland

Stadhouder William III

When the Stuarts yet returned to the throne of England in 1660, the position of the Oranges in the Republic was reinforced, and the 'Act of Seclusion' revoked, partly due to pressure by the new English king, Charles II, a cousin of young William III. For obvious political reasons, the States of Holland softened their anti-Orange attitude and even, quite politically, offered to undertake the education of the prince, now ten years old. In 1666 he became a 'ward of state'. Nevertheless, Johan de Witt wanted to restrict the influence of William's maternal relatives, the Stuarts, to a minimum if only because, by that time, the Republic again was at war with England, which in 1664 had taken New Amsterdam from the West India Company.

This second Anglo-Dutch war ended in a resounding success for the Dutch fleet under Admiral Michiel de Ruyter, who now became a national hero, as celebrated in folk song as was Piet Heyn. When he died, he was given a marble tomb in the Amsterdam New Church, situated where, in a Catholic church, the altar with the major saint would have been venerated.

While the Dutch destroyed a large part of the English fleet during a raid on the Medway, near London, and even captured the flagship 'Royal Charles', this victory at sea was largely due to the efforts of De Witt. He had secured adequate finance for the maintenance of a strong, well-equipped fleet. Obviously, this Dutch success helped to tone down the terms of the Navigation Act in the ensuing peace treaty.

Grand Pensionary Johan de Witt

As had happened with Oldenbarnevelt, De Witt, too, fell victim to the ambition and drive of a prince of Orange. While De Witt had done his best to build up the fleet, he had neglected the army. The danger of this policy became apparent in 1672 when French intrigue prompted England and the independent Catholic principalities of Munster and Cologne, the Republic's neighbours to the east, to join France and declare war on the Republic, all within one month. Soon, the entire south-eastern region of the Northern Netherlands was occupied by enemy troops. The people and some of the regents felt a military man capable of inspiring confidence in the population was needed; they now turned to the prince of Orange. Within two months, William was appointed stadhouder in all the provinces, except Friesland, where members of the Nassau family continued to hold the post they had acquired in the late sixteenth century. Moreover, William was also proclaimed captain-general and admiral-general.

De Witt had already admitted defeat by resigning his post when the French invaded, but now he and his brother were lynched and killed by a furious mob in The Hague. The ringleaders were not punished for this shameful deed; on the contrary, they were rewarded by the prince of Orange, though he may not have personally instigated them to this act.

Portrait of Grand
Pensionary Johan de
Witt (1625–1672)
RMA

The struggle for a balance of power in Europe

As soon as he was appointed captain-general, William III began to re-organize the neglected Dutch army. In 1647, admiral De Ruyter's victories at sea again forced England to come to terms with the Dutch. William's own military successes in the field led to peace with Munster and Cologne, leaving France the sole enemy. To some, the war, that continued to be waged until 1678, increasingly seemed like a matter of personal and dynastic prestige in which, according to William's critics, the interests of the Republic took second place behind those of the Orange family and the Prince's ego. However, to William it was a war that had to be waged and won in order to create a balance of power in Europe, to prevent France, which had been increasing its territory by conquest all along its borders, from achieving supreme hegemony. Only thus, he felt, could he secure continued independence for the Dutch. This concept was modern to the extent that it became a determining feature in many of the Republic's subsequent wars and was, indeed, adopted by many other states as well.

Meanwhile, as in 1648 the regents soon did see no more point in prolonging a costly war that damaged their commercial interests in France.

For the English their hour of direst need, for the Dutch a moment of victory: Admiral Michiel de Ruyter brings his fleet into the Thames and fights the battle of Chatham, 1666

Admiral Michiel
Adriaanszoon de Ruyter
(1606–1676)

Therefore, they urged the Stadhouder to come to terms with King Louis XIV. To the fury and disappointment of William, a peace treaty was negotiated at Nijmegen in 1678.

However, William eventually succeeded in reconciling the Republic to his grand design. His marriage to another Mary Stuart, his niece, for the daughter of James II of England, enabled him to become king of England, Scotland and Ireland in 1689, after his father-in-law had fled the country, leaving it in a state of political and religious turmoil. William then realised his fervent desire to create a grand alliance against France in which England, Spain, the Republic, the German Emperor, and some of the German principalities were united. Meanwhile, Louis XIV had taken the side of James II in his attempt to regain the throne, but his main aim was to conquer both the Spanish Netherlands and the Republic itself. This marked the outbreak of a Nine Years' War between France and the anti-French coalition.

William decided the Dutch should provide most of the resources for the war on land, while the English were to take the lead at sea. In so doing, he unwittingly created a situation in which the maritime supremacy of the English both during the war and during the subsequent years of peace grew ever stronger. In the long run, it was one of the reasons that caused the Republic to lose its erstwhile leading position in world trade.

For many years, France proved strongest in combat on land, but at sea it was no match for the combined English and Dutch fleets. The war dragged on without a final victory for either side until France's interest in the War of the Spanish Succession, which Louis hoped to win to enable his family to occupy the Spanish throne, took precedence over his wish to possess the Southern Netherlands. The Peace of Rijswijk was signed in 1697, allowing the Republic to garrison a number of fortress towns in the south, as a barrier against the inimical French.

Europe around the
conference table: the
ambassadors of the
European states trying
to negotiate peace
treaties at Nijmegen,
1676–1678

19 Society, politics and the economy in the late seventeenth and the eighteenth century

Although the seventeenth and eighteenth century have long been described as two contrasting periods in Dutch history, many eighteenth-century developments originated in the second half of the preceding century. Moreover, the alleged sudden decline of the Dutch Republic on all fronts of the economy and of culture is a fable. What happened was, rather, that a gradual change in the economic and social climate, from vigorous and progressive to conservative manifested itself. There was no longer a need to claim centre stage in the arena of European politics: at, admittedly, enormous costs, the Republic had succeeded in safeguarding its interests. The wish to preserve the status quo now became stronger. Yet, the Dutch continued to play an important role in world trade and through their investments retained their hold over international finance. But even though there was no noticeable overall economic decline, competition from other countries, notably England and France, now prevented the country to retain the near-monopoly it had held for nearly a century.

Progress and decline

In the early part of the seventeenth century, many wealthy merchants had invested in imaginative and even grandiose projects involving trade, industry and agriculture. The reclamation of land in the province of Holland to expand dairy farming was financed mainly from trade profits. In this way, one enterprise led to another. But in the eighteenth century investments were more often made abroad, especially in England and the Americas.

Dutch international trade did not begin to fail until fairly late in the eighteenth-century, but manufacture began to decline earlier. Partly in consequence of the high wages paid in the Netherlands, production in, for example, the textile industry at Leiden dropped by 80% between 1670 and 1795. Shipbuilding too, which had flourished in the Golden Age, was now in recession.

Declining investment in domestic enterprise and, again, the relatively generous wages customary in the Republic also resulted in a high level of structural unemployment and poverty among the industrial part of the population. As the small group of major investors grew wealthier, the social contrasts became greater than they had been in the preceding centuries.

The regents and state government until 1747

Another cause of the widening gap between social groups was the concentration of power in the hands of a few leading families, both in the towns and in the country. There had been urban oligarchies in the seven-

Four trustees of the Lepers' Asylum at Amsterdam (1773)
RMA

teenth century, but it had still been possible for new men and, later, their families to join the circle of regents, while others disappeared. In the eighteenth century such upward mobility became much harder. In almost all towns the majority of offices, from the highest to the most humble, were actually controlled by a few families. They drew up mutual agreements, so-called 'contracts of correspondence', promising not to appoint anyone from outside their closed circle to any post. Agreements of this kind led to the appointment of newborn babies to offices that were then filled by substitutes who were paid a fraction of the actual salary. Inevitably, this form of blatant nepotism and patronage bred corruption. It also caused growing dissatisfaction among the non-governing elite: the well-educated, wealthy patricians and prosperous bourgeois men who did not belong to the hallowed family circles that ruled the towns but felt they had every right to aspire to positions of power as well.

The increasing conservatism of the regents also influenced foreign policy. During the War of the Spanish Succession (1702-1713), Grand Pensionary Anthony Heinsius of Holland carried on the policy of William III to curb the power of France. But once the Treaty of Utrecht had been signed in 1713, giving France what it wanted in Spain, many political leaders felt there was no further need to actively take part in foreign affairs, the more so as continued involvement in military action obviously was very costly. Because of this, the Republic failed to play a significant role on the international stage and consequently lost much of its erstwhile prestige and power.

The reason for this indifference was, partly, the fact that by the time the Utrecht Treaty was signed, the Dutch Republic's treasury was almost empty. Moreover, the public debt, especially of Holland, had risen to such gigantic proportions that the economy was seriously affected. It was necessary to improve matters, among other things in the field of taxation, which had become chaotic. Adolf Hendrik, count of Rechteren, called for a Grand Assembly to be held at The Hague in 1716, for the second time in the history of the Republic. At this meeting, the secretary of the Council of State, Simon van Slingelandt, who was responsible for running the Union, proposed radical governmental reforms. The highly complex system of decision making, by which the delegates of the seven sovereign provinces had to consult their colleagues at home on every proposal put forward in the States-General, led to endless delays. But as the delegates at the Grand Assembly were subject to the same consultations, no agreement was reached and everything continued as before.

The Second Stadhouderless Period 1702–1747

When William III died in 1702, it seemed the House of Orange had no further part to play, as he had been the last direct male descendant of William the Silent. The title of prince of Orange passed to the Frisian line of the Nassau family, descending from one of William the Silent's brothers. But Johan Willem Friso of Nassau, stadhouder of Friesland and Groningen, died in an accident in 1711. His widow, Maria Louise of Hessen-Kassel, governed for their son Willem Karel Hendrik Friso, who had been born posthumously. In doing so, she won widespread respect with the result that, when William came of age, he was able to take his place as stadhouder in these two provinces without opposition. Soon, Gelderland also accepted him. However, the remaining four provinces, led by Holland, chose to continue this second Stadhouderless Period. William's marriage in 1734 to Anne, daughter of the new, Hanoverian king of England, illustrates the importance still accorded to the title and status of the Dutch stadhouder abroad.

It was not until 1747, when the Republic became involved in the European war over the Austrian Succession, and invasion by French troops was imminent that, just as in 1672, the prince of Orange, the Frisian Stadhouder William IV, was invited to become stadhouder in Holland, Zeeland, Utrecht and Overijssel as well. The background to the Republic's involvement in this war was a complicated one. It resulted from the Treaty of Vienna that had been signed in 1731. This agreement between Austria, England, Spain and the Republic had important political and economic aspects. The countries involved acknowledged the right of Maria Theresia, daughter of the emperor, to inherit all the Habsburg lands, which, since the Spanish Succession had been settled in 1713, also included the Southern, or Austrian Netherlands. Now, for signing the treaty, the Republic did ask a price: the Ostend Company, established in the Southern Netherlands in 1722, had become a threat to the Dutch East India Company. The Hague demanded that it be dissolved.

However, when, on the death of her father in 1746, Maria Theresia actually did claim her rights, other pretenders stated theirs as well. In the subsequent European war, the Republic was bound by the Vienna Treaty to furnish troops, but it waited so long in doing so that it lost much of the respect it still retained. Moreover, the new king of France declared war on the Republic, England and Austria in 1744, and French troops actually did invade the Southern Netherlands, also capturing some of the fortified barrier towns. By 1746, the Austrian Netherlands were almost entirely in the hands of the French. More threateningly, the Dutch part of Flanders was occupied in 1747.

William IV of Nassau, prince of Orange (1711–1751). Invested with great power, he yet disappointed many of his followers
RMA

The House of Orange: William IV and William V as hereditary stadhouders in all the provinces

Thus, in 1747, the threat of war as well as the dissatisfaction with the rule of an ever more closed regent oligarchy that had been mounting over the preceding decades resulted in more or less spontaneous popular rebellions in many of the towns, some of them orchestrated by the partisans of the Orange-family. Many people now asked for the recognition of William IV as hereditary stadhouder in all provinces. Encouraged by this, wealthy non-regent burghers took the opportunity of seizing power by joining the cause of the Prince. Yet they were Orangists for political reasons, only. Primarily, they regarded themselves as loyal to the 'Fatherland', and therefore have been named 'Patriots'.

In the following year 1748, the Treaty of Aix-la-Chapelle ended the war. William IV, safely installed in all provinces, now was free to deal with the many forms of corruption in the administration of the Republic. He even was authorized to appoint regents at the local, regional and national level. But instead of doing away with the abuses of the previous decades, he only took the opportunity of appointing his cronies wherever he could. This was a bitter disappointment to many of his supporters, who felt cheated in their own interests or realized that the reforms necessary to uphold the Republic's strength were not forthcoming.

In Amsterdam, serious rioting occurred in 1748 when the 'Doelisten', taking their name from the hall where they used to meet, voiced their demands. These included open access to public office, restoration of the privileges of the guilds and the allocation of the high proceeds from the postal service to the town rather than to a few families' private purses. William IV came to Amsterdam in person and agreed to the demands. But it was not long before things resumed their old course, which induced many educated non-regent burghers to unite and voice ever more radical political ideas, though these did not yet include any reference to such issues as sovereignty for the people on the basis of general suffrage.

A new political group now emerged, a modern-style 'party' almost, formed both by men from the old regent aristocracy who had fallen from grace in 1747, and by members of the wealthy bourgeoisie who still had no say in politics and government. Though they ultimately had different goals, for the time being they shared their dissatisfaction with the stadhouder's administration that was more domineering than ever. This party also called itself 'Patriotic', but it differed from its namesake of 1747 in that it was decidedly anti-Orangist. Their main aim was the constitutional reform of the decayed administrative system.

On the death of William IV in 1751, his widow ruled during the minority of their son William V, with the German Duke of Brunswick acting as captain-general. After having served the emperor, he had been engaged to reorganize the Republic's army and had gained great influence with the Orange family. The following years saw a bitter struggle between Amsterdam and William V, now of age, over the question whether to spend tax money on the equipment of the army or on building-up the fleet again. As usual, the Orange-party favoured the army, as it would strengthen the prince's position, while commercial Amsterdam supported the fleet, which it needed to regain some of the sea power the Dutch had lost to the British. Only in 1777, when Britain went to war against her American colonies, the Republic finally decided to equip twenty men-of-war.

The support then given to the American rebels by the more democratic-minded amongst the Dutch did not improve relations between the Republic and England. The decision of the States-General to provide convoys for the protection of the merchant fleet made matters worse. In December 1780, the fourth Anglo-Dutch War broke out, during which the superior British navy seriously damaged Dutch maritime trade.

William V of Nassau, prince of Orange (1748–1806), who came nearest to be the real ruler of the Dutch Republic, and yet failed to take the opportunity
RMA

Portrait by G. Haag of
William V of Nassau,
prince of Orange (1748–
1806), with his family
RMA

Patriots and Orangists

The political differences between Patriots and Orangists now emerged fully, as the former blamed Prince William V for this naval disaster because he, or at least his counsellors, always had opposed enlarging the fleet. In 1781, an anonymous pamphlet was distributed outlining Patriot ideology. It was addressed 'To the people of the Netherlands', and had been written by Johan Derk van der Capellen tot den Poll, a nobleman from Overijssel. He asked for constitutional reform but also advocated the establishment of a volunteer militia of armed civic guards. In the following years, such militias were duly mustered in many towns.

During this period, party politics became more articulate. All kinds of political demands both were more theoretically refined than ever before and, moreover, sounded a really revolutionary note, asking for reform in terms not of provincial sovereignty, only, but as something that should affect and alter the entire country. A sense of Dutch nationhood, rather than of Hollandish, Frisian or other regional feelings now emerged. Patriots from all over the Republic met to draw up a party manifesto. Patriotic newspapers such as the 'Post of the Lower-Rhine' were instrumental in this - a new cultural and political phenomenon as well, and one that was to become and remain a powerful force in shaping Dutch public opinion ever since. In 1784, this newspaper exposed the existence of the 'Consultation Act', an agreement between the Duke of Brunswick and William V, signed in 1766 when the Prince had just come of age. In it, William assured the Duke that the latter was only answerable to him for any advice he might give him in the future. This news raised a huge public outcry. Though by then Brunswick had left the country, the anti-Orange mood deepened.

The Patriot Movement found further inspiration in the American colonists' successful struggle for independence. At a congress of volunteer militiamen it was decided the Republic, too, should have a representative government. Some of the Patriots already drafted a new constitution closely resembling the American Declaration of Independence. This created a historically interesting situation, in that many of the American politicians themselves had gained some of their inspiration from republican theories and practices as expressed in the Netherlands in their own struggle for independence during the late sixteenth and early seventeenth century.

The Province of Utrecht, always a Catholic stronghold, and, moreover, with a capital where the traditions of the guilds were still respected, now became the centre of the Patriot Movement. However, when a democratic administration was formed there in 1786, due to the different social and political backgrounds of the Patriots a rift became apparent. The regents dismissed in 1747 only favoured abolishing the system of patronage as practised by the House of Orange. They definitely would not agree to the far-reaching plans for reform drawn up by the burgher-Patriots.

Though anti-Orange feeling rose high, and the provincial assemblies in Holland, Zeeland, Groningen and Overijssel even suspended Prince William as captain-general in 1786, the Stadhouder still remained popular with the general public. However, due to some rather foolish moves that further undermined his position, in 1787 he felt forced to call on his brother-in-law, the king of Prussia, to intervene on his behalf and reinstate him in his former power. This act of force was successful. The States of Holland were compelled to reverse all anti-Orange measures. But public dissatisfaction increased. Moreover, many Patriots fled to France, from where they continued their struggle with renewed vigour. They drew increasing sympathy, as William's reliance on foreign support and the way he tried to oust all political opponents in the following years was deeply resented.

The Duke of Brunswick-Wolfenbüttel (1718–1788), considered by many the 'evil genius' of William V

Noordbrabants Museum

20 Culture in the late seventeenth century and in the eighteenth century

Flowering and consolidation

During the first half of the seventeenth century, the Dutch Republic had experienced a marked flourishing of all fields of culture. The last decades of the century were rather less spectacular, as though Dutch culture had lost some of its sparkle. Elite culture now moved to the countryside, as many wealthy merchants bought country houses, some with manorial rights and titles - being mere burghers, they yet liked to ape the nobles who ruled the other European states. Life in the country was idealized, especially in the literary work of the second half of the century. In painting, idyllic landscapes were already popular in the 1640s: Jan Both (1618-1652) and Nicholaes Berchem (1620-1683) worked in this genre. At the same time, there was a general trend towards a frenchification of civilization among the upper classes. It was fashionable to speak French, and French tastes in clothing and food were adopted. Of course, this wish for social distinction was due to the influence of the glittering court of King Louis XIV at Versailles, that had become the cultural centre of Europe in the last decades of the seventeenth century. Around c. 1680, its undoubted splendour came to influence culture in all the surrounding countries.

Architecture and interior decoration

After 1685, when Louis reneged on his promise of religious freedom for the French Protestants, the arrival of numerous Huguenots, many of them able craftsmen and artists, also contributed to the introduction of French styles of architecture, interior decoration and furnishings in the Netherlands. Daniel Marot (1663-1752) was one of the newcomers. An engraver and interior decorator, he later worked as an architect as well. While he was employed at the court of William III, he designed the interior of the new Loo-palace, near Apeldoorn, the major remaining domestic baroque structure of the Netherlands. Comprehensive designs for entire interiors were new to the Republic and Marot and his followers set the trend. They also influenced the taste for decoration among the middle class and even well-to-do farming households all over the country until well into the twentieth century. Thus, the beautifully painted interiors and furnishings of houses at the town of Hindeloopen in Friesland and in the Zaan-region in North Holland, were imitations of the style popular at court and in stately homes at the beginning of the eighteenth century. Marot also designed the Huguetan-mansion at The Hague in a delicate baroque style, later repeated by other architects.

During the eighteenth century, new styles of architecture and decoration evolved or were adopted from abroad. Thus, a Dutch variant of the Rococo-style became popular in interior decoration. But when Leendert

Viervant designed a country house known as 'the Pavilion' for the wealthy banker and art-collector Henry Hope in Haarlem, he used the then newly fashionable neo-Classicist style.

The bedroom of Queen Mary of England, wife of Prince William III, at the Loo Palace. The interior has been restored by Daniel Marot

'The Pavilion', the Haarlem country house of the banker and art-collector Henry Hope, designed by Abraham van der Hart in the neo-Classicist style popular all over Europe

Provinciaal bestuur Noord-Holland, Haarlem

Painting

In a sense, painting suffered most from the widening gap between the various social groups. At the beginning of the seventeenth century, art, at least partly, still reflected the life of ordinary folk, which served as a colourful source of inspiration for genre painting. But this kind of work was not in demand with the people who bought or commissioned paintings in the eighteenth century. Bourgeois complacency looks out at us from the eighteenth century paintings by Wijbrand Hendriks (1744-1831), Adriaan de Lelie (1755-1820) and Jan Ekels (1759-1793), the only high-lights being the work of Cornelis Troost (1697-1750).

The grand tradition of Dutch painting also was influenced by the French taste in interior decoration. Walls were covered with decorative stucco and wallpaper; this left little space for pictures, certainly not large-scaled ones. As a result, however, the art of wallpaper painting flourished in the second half of the eighteenth century. It was fashionable to depict either scenes from China and Japan (which became a veritable craze), or of refined pastoral life, perhaps reflecting the anxieties induced by an increasingly urban society. Unfortunately, as fashions have changed again, since, most of this work has disappeared.

The inspectors of the
Amsterdam Collegium
Medicum (1724)
RMA

Literature

Wealthy burghers, rather more than patrons from the regent group, now dominated creative literature. An example is the

'Society for Dutch Literature', founded at Leiden in 1766. The members held monthly meetings to discuss their own work; they also maintained a library and reading room with national and international books. Initially, French taste also prevailed in literature - Voltaire's plays were hugely popular - and the resulting work was less than outstanding. However, many more people now became avid readers, aided by the number of journals of a general cultural nature published in the Republic. Though these mostly were written in French, they did help to spread the results of literary and scientific research and other cultural endeavours among a larger audience.

By the last decades of the century, the tentative beginnings of a new literary style appeared, less French-orientated both stylistically and as to its subject matter. Life in Dutch middle-class society was represented in a lightly satirical vein, especially in the work of Elisabeth Wolff (1738-1804), who, after her husband had died, shared home with Agatha Deken (1741-1804). Together, they wrote several successful epistolary novels, following the example of the English author Samuel Richardson. The best known and most readable of these is *Sara Burgerhart*, which was published in 1782.

Another author looking for new ways was the Leiden city administrator Hieronymus van Alphen (1746-1803). To the general public, he is best known for his children's verse, which opens up a window to changing ideas about marriage and family life, as well as to new didactic and pedagogical ideas. However, he was a versatile writer and influential cultural journalist, too, as shown in his tract on aesthetics.

Elisabeth Wolff (1738–
1804) and Agatha
Deken (1741–1804),
joint authors of the
famous epistolary
novel 'Sara Burgerhart'
(1782)
Iconografisch Bureau
Den Haag

Well-to-do Amsterdam
burghers taking art
classes

Science and religion

In addition to their increased involvement in literature, educated Dutch burghers also became interested in the natural sciences. This was in keeping with the rationalist outlook on life that had been growing since the late seventeenth century. The sciences were deemed particularly important since they promised spectacular technological and hence economic improvements. The 'Dutch Society for Science' was founded at Haarlem in 1752 to stimulate research. It periodically invited competitive essays on a variety of scientific and other subjects, often setting specific problems that, if solved, might lead to industrial application or other practical results. Similar societies were formed in other towns. The members, who stemmed from regent and well-to-do burgher circles alike, joined together in reading and commenting on scientific books, watching physical experiments or even performing them themselves.

Rationalist thinking also was applied to religious matters. Increasingly, people, while still believing the world originally had been created by God, yet held that it had continued to develop along independent lines. Soon, there was considerable support for this view in Dutch educated circles, leading to all kinds of religious speculation and, though perhaps not yet widely, to a new spirit of free thinking that also came to question traditional authority in both Church and State. Actually, recent research has shown that these new ideas, rather than being imported from abroad, had originated in the Dutch Republic itself. There, from the late seventeenth century onwards, a shift in the outlook on all aspects of human life had been taking place that preceded developments in eighteenth-century France. Indeed, the influence of this 'Dutch Enlightenment', both moderate and radical, on culture in other parts of Europe should not be underestimated.

21   Society and politics 1787–1815: revolt and foreign rule

Despite the developments sketched above, by the end of the eighteenth century inflexibility had come to characterize so many aspects of the life of the traditional elite of the Republic that the rise of even more radical ideas was inevitable. The gap between the well-to-do burghers and the lower classes mentioned above was one of the problems. The dissatisfaction of many educated people with the power monopoly of the ruling elite was another. But while a revolutionary spirit based on 'enlightened' ideas that became manifest in North America and France at the end of the eighteenth century was alive in the Republic, too, grumbling Dutchmen lacked the solidarity to bring about a real change. The populace, who were instrumental in bringing the revolution in France to its first successes, in the Dutch Republic were mainly of an Orangist persuasion and, hence, little inclined to alter the status quo.

The Batavian Republic 1795–1806

Indeed, in 1787 a revolt against the power of William V was crushed, at least for the time being. In the following year, all regents had to swear allegiance to the constitution, and the provinces agreed to maintain the position of the stadhouder.

When, as a consequence of the revolutionary developments in France, French troops invaded and occupied a large part of the Republic in 1795, this was partly at the instigation of the Patriots who had fled to Paris in 1787. The French soldiers hoped to strengthen their own revolution by attacking their foreign enemies, among whom they counted the traditionally pro-English Orangist party. Headed by Rutger Jan Schimmelpenninck (1761-1825), a group of Dutchmen in favour of reform now took the opportunity of seizing power. A new, so-called Batavian Republic was proclaimed. Prince William V fled to England, never to return.

To enact constitutional reforms, elections were held for a National Assembly to replace the States-General. All males over the age of 20 and of fixed abode were eligible to vote if they were not dependent on charity. Another condition was that they had to abjure the stadhouder-system.

The first session of the first Dutch National Assembly (1796)

Rutger Jan
Schimmelpenninck
(1761–1825), Grand
Pensionary of the
Batavian Republic from
1805 till 1806
RMA

The first meeting of the National Assembly was held on 1 March 1796. Soon, a committee was formed to draft a new constitution. But the Assembly proved to be divided by a bitter controversy between federalists, who were in favour of maintaining provincial independence, and Unitarians, who were against it and wanted a centralized state, arguing that for more than a century already the Dutch Republic had failed to function properly precisely because it had remained an ineffective confederation of seven small states loosely linked by the provisions of the Union of Utrecht.

After much bickering, a constitution based on Unitarian principles was adopted in April 1798. It divided the country into eight departments. Local and departmental authorities were to be elected by those eligible to vote. The same applied to the Legislative Assembly, a national body with the power to appoint an Executive Council of five directors. The new constitution became effective during the same year. The strange polity that for two hundred years had been the Republic of the Seven United Dutch Provinces ceased to exist.

The new order soon materialised in a variety of decisions. In 1798, a separation between State and Church was effectuated, which opened the way to the legal equality of all denominations and religions. Especially the Roman Catholics and the Jews were now given the right to once more worship in public. Gradually, a number of fiscal and legal measures, and the parallel centralization of government paved the way for further development towards national unity. Still, the new Dutch state functioned under French supervision, only.

Indeed, in 1801 a coup was staged by the French military commander, General Augereau, with the help of three members of the Executive Council, to bring the Republic even more into line with France's by now heavily anti-English policy, willed by Napoleon Bonaparte. Consequently, a new constitution was implemented which on some points recreated the situation that had existed before 1795.

In 1805, however, consultations had to be held between Napoleon and Schimmelpenninck, the new Dutch envoy in Paris. For the French dictator-turned-emperor now favoured the introduction of a single ruler, wholly dependent on him, hoping this would strengthen Dutch support in the French struggle against England. Schimmelpenninck returned to the Netherlands to present the voters with a draft constitution granting executive power to a new official, typically to be called 'pensionary', showing people still thought in terms reminiscent of the Dutch 'old regime'. He himself would be the first to hold this office. There also was to be a Legislative Assembly of 19 members authorized to appoint this pensionary and with the right to vote bills.

Schimmelpenninck could count on the help of several able ministers and with them pursued a fairly progressive policy. National regulations for elementary education were provided for the first time in the Education Act of 1806. Responsibility for education now lay with the state instead of the town councils, the Churches or private schools. Teacher training was instituted as well to guarantee a certain quality of education.

Unfortunately, Schimmelpenninck had to resign his office after only a year when, in 1806, Napoleon, still dissatisfied with the Batavian Republic's according to him ineffective support of the French Empire's war effort, decided to re-establish it as a kingdom, with his youngest and favourite brother Louis Napoleon Bonaparte as its sovereign.

Meanwhile, the economy of the Netherlands had declined steadily. During the last quarter of the eighteenth century, the Dutch East India Company had suffered such heavy losses that it had to be liquidated in 1795. In 1798, the Batavian Republic took over its debts and assets, and on 31 December 1799 this renowned and once very successful Dutch multinational ceased to exist. The West India Company already had been dismantled in 1791.

Soon, however, France imposed the so-called 'continental system' on all its dependent states, in order to block commerce with England. This meant Dutch overseas trade became virtually impossible, a disaster for a country that for centuries had thrived on it. Moreover, the alliance of the former Republic, now the Kingdom of Holland, with France involved it ever more closely in the French wars with Great Britain. The United Kingdom saw its chance to occupy the profitable Dutch trading posts in Asia, one by one. While some of these were returned to the Netherlands in 1814, at the London Convention, the most lucrative ones were retained by England.

Dutch industry, too, was in a poor state. Small-scale business accounted for most of the production. Such technical innovations as introduced in the British textile industry yet were lacking. The majority of the wealthy burghers were little inclined to finance innovations, if only because they had been forced to accept a severe loss on their investments after the national debt was reduced to a third of its value following the annexation of the Netherlands by France.

The Kingdom of Holland under Louis Napoleon Bonaparte, 1806–1810

Rather surprisingly, the new king 'of Holland' soon grew to actually love his kingdom, or perhaps rather his role, to the extent that his imperial brother quickly became wary of his enthusiasm, which did not seem to prioritize the French interests. Certainly, Louis's government was not unbeneficial to the Netherlands. In many fields it pursued the centralizing, rational policy adopted in the preceding years, and provided new stimuli, specifically in fiscal reorganization, water management and the improvement of infrastructure. Of

Louis Napoleon Bonaparte (1778–1846), from 1806–1810 first king of Holland, by C. Hodges.
To a large extent, King Louis laid the foundations for the monarchy that later was vested in the House of Orange
RMA

King Louis arrives in
Amsterdam
JHM

Undated letter of a
Frisian soldier who had
been drafted for the
Napoleonic army, to
his fiancée

Tresoar Leeuwarden

undeniable importance was the introduction, in 1808, of a new civil code, following French lines, which soon greatly influenced life in all its legal aspects, the more so as precisely in this respect the seven provinces had been hopelessly divided. In 1810, the system of local registry offices was adopted for the compulsory registration of births, deaths and marriages, which, of course, was to prove of great help to the government's fiscal-economic policies. Many Dutch families now took or were given a surname for the first time.

King Louis also encouraged a number of important cultural developments. In 1808, the Royal Institute of Science, Literature and the Arts was founded at his instigation. One of its tasks was to organize an exhibition of works by contemporary Dutch artists, to be held every other year. This certainly stimulated cultural life in various ways. The monarch also paved the way for the foundation of the later 'Rijksmuseum', establishing a Royal Museum in part of the old town hall of Amsterdam, which he had taken for his palace. Although most of the works he showed there came from the former stadhouder's collection, the King took great pleasure in royally adding to it. For instance, he included Rembrandt's 'Night Watch', that still belonged to the city of Amsterdam, though even now it was not to the taste of the time, yet. In creating the museum, Louis gave the Netherlands a temple wherein to glorify their national cultural and historical memories. He thus enabled the Dutch to experience their past and, indeed, see it as a great past, a Golden Age. In a sense, it helped them on the way towards nationhood, towards a common identity.

However, in 1809, Louis's reign was cut short by the unsuccessful English invasion of Zeeland, which led to the arrival of French troops. Though the first Dutch king even attempted to defend the country entrusted to him against the army sent by his brother, the Emperor, the majority of the Dutch people did not dare support him. In 1810, he abdicated in favour of his second son, whom, however, his imperial uncle did not allow to take

the throne.

The Netherlands annexed by and opposed to France, 1810–1813

By 1810, Napoleon had already decided to annexe the Netherlands to France, thus realizing a very old French ambition, viz. dominion over the Rhine Delta and, through it, over much of the commercial contacts between the North Sea and Central Europe.

Soon, conscription, determined by lot, was introduced to bring Napoleon's 'Grand Army' up to strength - precisely the army he needed to fight off the people who, all over Europe, opposed his enlightened but, by many, deeply resented regime. As a result, nearly 15,000 Dutch soldiers were forced to accompany the Emperor on his ill-fated Russian campaign in the following year, 1812. Very few of them survived this terrible experience.

This, and the economic recession which set in when the Netherlands were forbidden to trade with England or non-European countries, caused anti-French feelings to run high. As always in a crisis, many, though certainly not all Dutchmen turned to the House of Orange once more. In 1813, the defeat of Napoleon by a European coalition at Leipzig signalled the retreat of French troops from Dutch soil. Three regents, Gijsbert van Hogendorp, Frans van der Duyn van Maasdam and Leopold van Limburg Stirum now took power, governing the land pending the return of the man they hoped might lead a once more independent state, viz. the oldest son of the last Orange-stadhouder, who had died in exile in England.

Prince William of Orange, son and heir of William I, the first Orange king, leading his regiment in the battle of Quatre Bras on 16 June 1815, painted by J.W. Pieneman
RMA

22 Society, politics, economy and culture in the Kingdom of the United Netherlands, 1815–1830/1839

The reunion of the Northern and Southern Netherlands: the constitution of 1815

Invited by the three interim rulers, the hereditary prince of Orange landed at Scheveningen on 30 November 1813. Although, in previous years, William VI of Orange (1772-1843) had tried to accommodate himself with Napoleon, even asking the French leader to appoint him his representative in the Netherlands, he now was inaugurated as the new sovereign at Amsterdam, on 2 December, styled William I. In 1814, he also accepted sovereignty over the Southern Netherlands that had been liberated from France as well and had not been returned to its former Austrian rulers.

In 1815, William proclaimed himself 'King of the Netherlands', thus reuniting the seventeen provinces after a separation of over 225 years. But the reunion was not destined to last, though people still argue over the reasons. Many hold that differences in economic life, religion, culture and politics simply had grown too great. Some even question whether the cohesion often claimed by the adherents of the so-called 'greater Netherlands-idea' ever had been a historical reality. For the seventeen Netherlands actually only had existed as a 'unity' because they had shared the same monarch, Emperor Charles V. And even that fragile union had lasted for a few decades, only, in the early years of the sixteenth century. Also, during the two centuries of its independent existence, the Republic of the Seven United Provinces itself had had serious problems in overcoming its own, internal differences. However, other historians feel the new kingdom might have stood a chance had not the new sovereign, however enthusiastic and capable, acted as an authoritarian, 'enlightened despot', proceeding along lines that, to many, accentuated rather than diminished the differences.

One of the points of friction soon dividing the new kingdom was the composition of the second chamber of Parliament. In the South, the population was larger than in the North, and yet each part was represented by 55 members. Meetings were held alternately at The Hague and Brussels. Soon, the Southern members, representing, moreover, a mainly Roman Catholic constituency, complained of strong discrimination and began to sabotage many of the government's proposals, though objectively seen these were for the common weal. The King now decided to rule by royal decree, mostly, which inevitably raised more opposition, now also from liberals and, indeed, both in the South and in the North. In 1828, this even resulted in a so-called 'unholy alliance' between Catholics and liberals.

One of the major political and cultural problems was denominational education, more specifically as provided by the religious Orders of the Roman Catholic Church, because it required governmental approval. As education in the South always had been the uncontested domain of the Church, this new policy was felt to be intolerably patronizing.

Language posed another problem. Both in the Walloon provinces such as Hainault and Liège, and amongst the upper class of Flanders, French was spoken. This very much accentuated existing socio-economic differences and power positions. Also, it was unacceptable to the new king's 'national' vision. Therefore, William I decreed that at least the civil service in the entire kingdom was to use Dutch, thus trying to speed up the unification of the two parts of the kingdom by creating one culture. Not unreasonably, he argued that having both Dutch and French would divide rather than unite.

Press censorship, too, caused trouble. People were taken to court for insulting the government or for voicing critical remarks about royal policy. While these restrictions pertained equally to critics in the North and in the South, they specifically added to the strain on the relations between William I and his southern subjects, that increased during the fifteen years following the reunion.

When an industrial crisis threatened in 1830, the southerners blamed the government for its free trade policy that, or so they felt, did not protect their largely industrial economy in any way, while the northern, trading economy was unduly favoured. By then, the situation in the South contained all the ingredients for an escalation of civic unrest. Also, foreign influences, specifically French and English, undermined William's position: France was decidedly unhappy once more to have lost its hold over the Southern Netherlands, while Britain, having helped to create the kingdom of the Netherlands to counterbalance French power, now felt it had also created an increasingly successful economic competitor.

William Frederic (1772–1843), who started as hereditary prince of Orange and later (1815) became King William I of the Netherlands
RMA

The establishment of the Belgian State: 1 October 1830

After some rioting and disturbances in Brussels and other places in the South in September 1830, dissatisfied southerners set up a temporary administration. An independent state called Belgium was proclaimed on the 1st of October and a national conference was convened.

In November, those foreign powers who were interested in the status of the Netherlands, including Russia, England, France, Prussia and Austria, met in London. Especially England, that in these very decades had been building its own position as a leading industrial nation, realized it did not exactly relish a territorially and economically strong 'greater' Netherlands, while the French had not yet lost their perennial aversion against an independent power on their northern borders. A month later, the Kingdom of the United Netherlands had been dissolved and in January 1831 the foundation of Belgium was formalized.

While King William, reluctantly, was prepared to accept the decisions of the London Conference, the Belgians felt slighted by some of the clauses. A later proposal, presented in June, was acceptable to the Belgians, but not to the monarch. Meanwhile, Leopold of Saxe-Coburg - perhaps not surprisingly closely related to the British royal family - had been elected king of the Belgians.

For the time being, William I persisted in refusing to accept the new proposals. In August, during the notorious 'Ten-Day Campaign', the Dutch army initially defeated the Belgians, but was forced to retreat when the French intervened. A truce was finally concluded in 1833, but only in 1838 did William I agree to the clauses drawn up by the London Conference. The final treaty, acceptable to all parties, was signed in 1839. It marked the end of the brief reunion of the Southern and Northern Netherlands. Since then, the North has been known as the Kingdom of the Netherlands, while the south is, officially, the Kingdom of the Belgians. Over the past nearly two centuries, the relationship between the two nations has improved, even to the extent that both in the north and in the south there are those who deplore the split and feel that a strong state would have been preferable after all.

William I, the 'Merchant-King': trade and industry

Though William I met with increasing resistance from parts of the population because of his high-handed behaviour, his contribution to economic revival in both North and South was tremendous. He deservedly earned his nickname of 'merchant-king' by his tireless efforts to restore prosperity to the Netherlands' trade and industry, though, admittedly, this policy helped him to amass a fortune as well.

One of his initiatives was to set up the Dutch Trading Company. William personally invested 4 million guilders in it - some hundreds of millions in present-day currency - and guaranteed the other shareholders a divi-

dend of 4% for the first 25 years. He then proceeded to try and help the Company to conquer the developing markets of the newly independent Latin American states, assuming, wrongly, that the Dutch would have easy access there, due to their colonial past. After 1830 the activities of the Trading Company were concentrated on dealing with the Netherlands East Indies, which had been returned to the Dutch, mostly because the English felt unable to actually hold on to it.

Sent there by King William, governor-general John van den Bosch introduced the 'cultivation system'. Native farmers were forced to use a fifth of their land to produce the crops ordered by the Dutch government. The products, such as coffee and sugar, were shipped to the Netherlands by the Dutch Trading Company and marketed both nationally and internationally. Return cargo consisted, among other things, of cotton textiles. In this way, Dutch industry was supplied with cheap raw materials and Dutch trade found a profitable outlet. Indeed, the cotton industry, initiated in the Twente-region of Overijssel in 1833, had been set up to manufacture textiles mainly for the Indian market. Its subsequent

success was partly due to the fact that by now the Belgian textile industry was no competitor anymore.

William I tried to stimulate the economy in many other ways as well. Thus, the Bank of the Netherlands and the State Mint were established on his instigation, to ensure government control of the money market. The gradual introduction of the metric system, though not an easy operation, while meant to favour a unified way of thinking in general, particularly benefited the economy. William also improved public transport by promoting large infrastructural works such as the building of roads and the construction of canals. The North Holland Canal, connecting the capital to the open sea, re-opened the port of Amsterdam to the large vessels that now carried European trade. At the end of William's reign, in 1839, the first of the Dutch railways was inaugurated, between Amsterdam and Haarlem.

Undeniably, private enterprise also was instrumental in making the Netherlands a great trading power once more. The Steamship Companies of Rotterdam and Amsterdam were founded in 1823 and 1825, respectively, and together created the modern Dutch shipbuilding industry.

But though the economy was gradually recovering, there was widespread poverty during the first decades of the nineteenth century. The so-called 'Relief Company' was founded in 1818 to combat this by providing employment for those unable to earn a living. In Drenthe, the development of wasteland was undertaken, to be used for agriculture and cattle breeding. The reclamation of one of the last remaining great lakes, the Haarlemmermeer, created the possibility to establish huge new farms as well. Plans even were made to reclaim the entire Zuiderzee. Yet, though of great economic importance, all these measures could not, of course, structurally eradicate poverty. Consequently, many who were dependent on, especially, agriculture, decided to leave their country and seek their fortune abroad. In the course of the nineteenth century, the United States of America, with its promise of unlimited possibilities, became the new fatherland of many Dutch families. Still, many immigrants continued to cling to their own culture for generations, specifically through their own schools and newspapers.

Culture and religion under William I

As indicated above, William definitely wanted to promote the Dutch language, to help create a common culture. Nevertheless, regional dialects, sometimes with very obvious linguistic characteristics of their own, survived. Consequently, regional cultures survived, especially in the rural areas, where the civilisation of the new, urban, industrial elite did not penetrate as yet.

In painting, too, the quest for national symbols was reflected. So-called history painting flourished, now taking its subjects from the, often idealized an mythicized history of the Netherlands in the sixteenth and seventeenth centuries. Indeed, it was only during the nineteenth century that this earlier period began to be viewed as the Dutch 'Golden Age' on which the people of the Netherlands looked back with, many would say, justifiable pride.

William's educational policy, though a problem in his linguistic and ecclesiastical relations with the South, was not without effect, either. In Delft, he established the Academy for Civil Engineering, to contribute both to economic life and to the needs of the military. It was one of the centres from which a new use of mathematics was propagated to help solve the problems of man and society by introducing well-reasoned arguing, an approach favoured by William's education ministers in other school types as well.

In the same spirit of building a national culture, William I wanted to turn the Dutch Reformed Church into a spiritual haven for every Dutchman. This, of course, while unacceptable to the Roman Catholics, also irked some dogmatically Calvinist movements, resulting in a schism in 1834. The government's very harsh reaction caused many of the followers of this puritan group to decide to emigrate to the U.S.A as well.

Meanwhile, though the law guaranteed freedom of religion to all, there was no real equality in this field as yet, which did not improve relations between specifically, the Protestant and the Roman Catholic parts of the Dutch population.

The King's abdication: 1840

After a controversial reign that had lasted 27 years, William I had alienated himself from many of his subjects by his self-willed policy, though he had worked wonders for the economy, promoting and developing prosperity all over the Netherlands. Public unrest - fuelled, it has to be said, by the king's eldest son - arose when, after the death of his first wife, Frederica of Prussia, William announced his intention to marry a Roman Catholic, and, moreover, Belgian noblewoman. In 1840 he decided to abdicate in favour of his son. He then left for Berlin, where he died in 1843.

King William I signs his act of abdication, 1840

The constitutional reforms of 1840 and 1848

In 1840, as a result of the independence of Belgium, constitutional reforms were necessary. Some of the leading liberals as well as some progressive Roman Catholic leaders saw their chance of effectuating a number of democratic changes. Most important of these was the introduction of ministerial responsibility. This would enable Parliament to call ministers to account for government policy, where formerly they reported to the king, only. Well aware of the fact that this would greatly restrict his power, King William II (r. 1840-1848) rejected the proposed reforms. He would only agree to the introduction of a limited form of ministerial responsibility, which held ministers accountable in case they acted against the law.

**William II (1792–1849)
King of the Netherlands
(1840–1849)**

During the following years, the government and the reformers were unable to reach an agreement. Only when the king was faced with the threat of revolution - which became a reality in many European states in 1848 - did he finally accept a more liberal constitution. Proclaimed on 3 November, the text had been drafted by a committee of which the Liberal leader Johan Rudolph Thorbecke (1798-1872) was a member.

The most important revisions concerned the central administration. Ministerial responsibility to Parliament was introduced, stipulating that, henceforth, 'the king could do no wrong'. From now on, members of the Upper Chamber, instead of being appointed by the sovereign, would be elected by the assemblies of the provinces. The Lower Chamber, as well as the provincial assemblies and the municipal councils were to be elected directly by the electorate. The right to vote was, however, restricted to those men who paid taxes; general male suffrage was not introduced, yet, nor, indeed, were women included. The Lower Chamber was given the rights of amendment, interpellation and enquiry. Also, it was ruled that all meetings of representative bodies were to be held in public.

Limiting royal power

The constitutional revision of 1848 reduced the political power of the monarch to a few, well-defined rights. One of these was the right to dissolve Parliament. In practice this only applied to the Lower Chamber, with the odd exception. It soon was clear that William II could not resign himself to these restrictions. However, his early death in the same year did not put him to the test of the changed circumstances. But his son William III (r. 1849-1890) had great problems in accepting this loss of royal power as well. Consequently, he constantly meddled in politics. In 1866, a clash of wills occurred as he dissolved both Chambers because he was reluctant to accept the resignation of the sitting government. He ordered new elections, and even advised the people to vote for a Parliament that would support the team he favoured. Though many politicians and citizens felt the King had hugely overstepped his constitutional limits, at first William had his way: the cabinet stayed on. But at the first opportunity the newly-elected Lower Chamber again expressed its disapproval of government policy. Once more, the government handed in its resignation, and once more the king dissolved the Chamber. After the elections, the liberals were strongly represented in the new Parliament. Consequently, William had to admit defeat and his cabinet was sent home. A new government led by the Liberal Thorbecke took its place. Since then, the Dutch monarchs have, by and large, accepted their position as a symbol of the unity of the Dutch people, although William III continued to find this irksome.

In 1890, the King was succeeded by his only surviving child, Wilhelmina. She inherited the crown due to the death of her three half-brothers, William's sons by his first wife. Acceding to the throne at the tender age of 10, her mother, Queen Emma, acted as a regent till she came of age. When she actually took on her responsibilities, she, too, found it difficult to comply with the rules of the constitutional game. Exercising considerable influence behind the scene - as have done her daughter and granddaughter after her - Queen Wilhelmina still was generally respected for the conscientious way in which she fulfilled her role. Specifically the vigorous stance she took, according to many, during the Second World War earned her a reputation which, finally, ensured her the epithet of 'mother of the fatherland'.

Meanwhile, in the period between 1840 and 1914, the Netherlands slowly developed from a predominantly agricultural society into an industrial one. In 1840, the year of William I's abdication, society was not yet on its way towards industrialization. True, the textile industry in Twente was flourishing, but there was no large-scale, heavy industry worth speaking of. However, in the following years the Dutch economy gradually developed towards a modern, industrial-capitalist system along liberal lines. Especially Thorbecke did much to stimulate the transition from a mercantilist to a free-trade policy.

Yet, around the 1850s, in the field of technology and engineering the Netherlands still lagged behind most of the industrialized European nations - Britain and parts of Germany first and foremost. The expansion of the railway system proceeded only slowly. It was not until the 1860s, when government decided to intervene, that construction was speeded up.

Portrait of the liberal statesman Johan Rudolph Thorbecke (1798–1872)

Inauguration of King
William II in the New
Church of Amsterdam
on 28 November 1840,
by N. Pieneman
RMA

Workers unite

Yet, industry gradually took the place of agriculture as the major sector of the economy. In the second half of the century, most manual labour was taken over by machines. As everywhere, in the beginning these developments harmed the position of many factory workers. Moreover, the liberal distaste of government intervention, as well as the reluctance on the entrepreneurs' part to invest in improved working conditions meant that workers' rights were hardly protected, if at all. When times turned bad, wages were lowered, without any kind of compensation; working hours always were long; child labour was regarded as normal.

Inevitably, people started protesting against the inhuman conditions in which they were forced to live and work. Initially, private initiative, such as displayed by the 'Society for the Common Weal', tried to combat social problems. Actions were undertaken against alcoholism, which was widespread, and the vocational training of girls and women, as yet poorly implemented, now was deemed opportune. In the course of the century, political groups such as the Socialists started helping workers to speak up. Soon, the labouring population decided to really unite in an effort to achieve better conditions. The Dutch General Workers' Union was formed in 1872. Significantly, however, at first it refused to use job actions as a means to effectuate socio-economic change: people as yet clung to a traditional view of the hallowed order of society. The Protestant Union, 'Patrimonium', founded in 1876, and the Roman Catholic Workers' Union, formed by the priest Alphons Ariens, held the same view.

At the beginning of the twentieth century, however, many felt that, if politicians and the economic elite would not move, they had to really act themselves. Indeed, when government formally attempted to prevent strikes by passing laws prohibiting civil servants to use this weapon as a form of protest, a railway strike broke out in 1903. A second walk-out, which was meant to be general, failed when it was called for. But though many workers still were hesitant to use these means, the social climate definitely changed.

The first social legislation

Strangely, the first real social law was not the work of Socialists or, even, organized workers. It was the liberal Member of Parliament Samuel van Houten who, in 1874, introduced a bill prohibiting child labour for those who were under twelve years of age. Slowly, people began to realize that the miserable circumstances in which many had to survive could no longer be tolerated. In 1886, the government ordered an inquiry into the condition of factory workers. Action did not follow immediately, but the inquiry itself was a sign of a new attitude to social problems. As a result, a number of laws were introduced in the following years which did lead to a general improvement in the position of the labouring class. The Factory Act was passed in 1889, prohibiting child labour altogether and, moreover, regulating working conditions for adolescents and for women. A system of factory inspection was introduced to ensure that these regulations were observed. Nevertheless, only when primary education became compulsory in 1900, a real stop was put to child labour.

Samuel van Houten hailed by the children whose lot his legislation improved

Emancipation of Roman Catholics and Jews

The constitution of 1848 had finally recognized the right of every Dutchman to freely worship. But the subsequent re-establishment of the Episcopal sees and, consequently, of the Catholic hierarchy in April 1853, after having been in abeyance for 250 years, brought furious protests from dogmatic Protestant circles. The violent reactions in favour of and against this so-called 'April Movement', shook the nation. Thorbecke's first cabinet fell over the affair. But emancipation of the Roman Catholics, still more than a third of the Dutch population, proceeded all the same, slowly but surely. Meanwhile, the Jews, by far the smaller group, and thus less of a threat to the ruling, Christian and Liberal elite and the prevailing religious-cultural climate, already had succeeded in securing themselves a better position.

Denominational and non-denominational education: the battle over the schools

The constitution of 1848 also had established people's right to choose their own schools. This gave rise to a fierce struggle over the financial equality of denominational and state education. Until then, only non-denominational, 'neutral' education had been funded by the government. A 'battle over the schools' resulted, in which both the Catholics and the Dutch Reformed communities began to tighten their organizations to enforce their right to have their own, state-financed form of education and, hence, of culture. Legislation was eventually passed in 1889 obliging the government to fund denominational education as well. However, full equality was not realized till the constitutional reform of 1917.

In 1863, Thorbecke also introduced a law on secondary education, resulting in the foundation of the so-called 'Higher Burgher School', or H.B.S. It was to replace the old-fashioned 'French Schools' and to provide training geared to a modern, industrial society. It catered, mainly, to the needs and aspirations of the prosperous bourgeoisie. However, like the traditional Latin schools, known as Gymnasiums since 1876, the 'Higher Burgher Schools' were soon preparing students for university education as well.

In this welter of socio- and religious-emancipatory movements, the women of the Netherlands now were heard for the first time, speaking up in defence of a fairer society in which they would no longer be regarded and treated as second-rate citizens.

William III (1817–1890), the least-loved of the three first Orange-kings (1849–1890)

Aletta Jacobs was an example to many: in 1870, she was the first girl to be admitted to the H.B.S., and she went on to complete her education at the university. She became the first female medical doctor in the Netherlands.

Ethical politics in relation to the colonies

Besides fundamentally altering many aspects of Dutch society at home, the constitution of 1848 also affected developments in the Dutch colonies. Until 1848, the monarch had ruled supreme in colonial affairs, both in the East and in the West. Now, this power, too, was taken from him. This meant a new form of government had to be set up in the Dutch East Indies. A new system also was introduced in the Antilles in 1865; and Surinam even was given an elected parliament of its own. Just as there was a heightened awareness of social problems in the Netherlands themselves, critics now realized that the colonies and their inhabitants were being exploited, too. In 1860, the writer Eduard Douwes Dekker protested under the name of 'Multatuli', i.e. 'I have suffered greatly', against the excesses of forced cultivation in the East Indies, in his famous novel: *Max Havelaar, or the coffee auctions of the Dutch Trading Company*. The outcry it caused was not in vain. The cultivation system was abolished a decade later, with the adoption of a 'Cultivation Act'. It enabled indigenous farmers to lease land from the Dutch government without the obligation of growing specific crops for the (European) export market.

Another step forward was taken when, in 1899, a sensational article titled 'A Debt of Honour' was published in the influential literary magazine *De Gids* (The Guide). It marked the beginning of the so-called 'ethical policy', favoured by those politicians who advocated a slow evolution to eventual self-rule for the colonies. Nevertheless, many years were to pass before this ideal was actually realised.

Since the seventeenth century, the Netherlands had participated in, and profited from the trading of slaves from Africa to the Americas, and had maintained slavery in its slave-driven plantation colony of Surinam. Consequently, the Netherlands had to take a stance in the international discussion over the abolition of the slave trade, and of the system of slavery itself in the Americas. While other European governments decided to change their policy, the Dutch held on to the system for an, in retrospect embarrassingly long time: slavery in the Duct colonies was only abolished in 1863. Inevitably, the economy of Surinam fell into a recession,

Stedman T. I. Tav. IV.

NEGRO SOSPESO VIVO PER LE COSTE.

Lazaretti colori

For many centuries, the Dutch maintained slavery in their American colonies

A slave market in Surinam, c. 1830

A. Kuyper (1837–1920), leader of the (Calvinist) Anti-Revolutionary Party

H. Schaepman (1844–1903), leader of the Roman Catholic Party

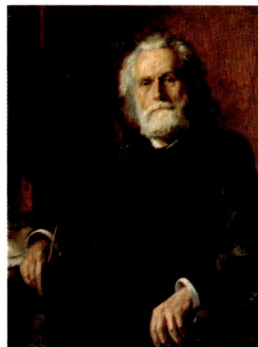

F. Domela Nieuwenhuis (1846–1919), the first Socialist member of Parliament

in spite of the arrival of Hindustani immigrants from British India, and of Javanese labourers from the Dutch East Indies - an immigration strongly stimulated by the Dutch government and, therefore, not to be considered entirely free. Meanwhile, the situation did contribute to the slow growth of a fascinating multi-cultural society in the West-Indian colony.

The rise of political parties

In the Netherlands, political parties in the modern sense began to form hesitantly around 1880, as a result of industrialization, social organization and the religious-political agitation surrounding legislation on education. The Anti-Revolutionary Party was founded in 1878, on the basis of a program written by the writer-politician and Protestant minister Abraham Kuyper. The Liberals organized themselves in the Liberal Union in 1885, adopting, however, a much less rigid footing. Already in 1883, a Roman Catholic leader, the priest Herman Schaepman had presented a political manifesto as well. However, it was not accepted by a majority of Catholic voters until 1896.

Though a Social-Democratic Union had been founded in 1881, the Socialists did not enter the political arena till 1888 when their leader, the former Lutheran preacher Ferdinand Domela Nieuwenhuis, became the first Socialist to be elected to the Lower Chamber, even though he had been in prison for 'lèse-majesté' only a year before.

'Pillarization'

One of the consequences of the emancipatory movements of the later nineteenth century was the way in which Dutch society became 'pillarized'. The term tries to capture the process in which the Dutch people now divided into a number of sharply distinct groups, or 'pillars', distinguished by their own characteristic religious and political ideas, which soon also came to determine the economic, social and cultural choices they made. In sports and in musical pastimes, in literature and in the arts, and even in the media - journals, and, later radio and television -, people organized themselves according to the dictates of their 'pillar': Catholic or Protestant, and, numerically to a far lesser extent, Liberal or Socialist. Priests and ministers, and non-religious political leaders gained great power over the hearts and minds of their communities. The majority of the Dutch remained deeply religious, or became even more so. Public morals were, if anything, even stricter than in 'Victorian England'. The amount of illegal births in the Netherlands was astonishingly low, as was the number of forced marriages and divorces, while, on the other hand, the birth rate was very high, especially in the Roman Catholic parts of the country.

In short, within Dutch, 'pillarized society', solid power blocks were constructed, with their own political parties, schools and professional organizations: separate worlds, with little contact between each other. Indeed, such a thing as an inter-denominational marriage was almost unthinkable. For while intellectuals in all groups tried to maintain some kind of national, non-partisan culture, sometimes even criticising their own 'pillar' for its conservative stance, Roman Catholic priests, Protestant ministers and Socialist politicians did not hesitate to use the pulpit or the stage to incite their flock to strictly adhere to their own culture.

The situation inevitably led to the call for general male suffrage. For 'pillarization' had given the political leaders a definite following who, if all were given the vote, could be used to support demands to improve at least the position of their own group. Paradoxically, however, this turned Dutch parliamentary democracy into a very consensual system: politics ever since have only been effective insofar as the various 'pillars' constantly tried to create coalitions that would ensure a workable government.

Between 1848 and 1887, the number of men eligible to vote by law was still small. In 1887, the constitution as well as the electoral system were reformed once more, giving the vote to every male who could prove financial independence and moral probity. Both Socialists and other radicals felt this reform did not go far enough: they favoured general male suffrage. Hence, in 1896, the number of voters rose to more than half of the adult male population as a result of yet another electoral reform. But general male suffrage was not adopted until 1917, and women had to wait for another two years.

King William III with his second wife, Queen Emma, and their only child, Wilhelmina, who had to save the Orange–monarchy from extinction

24 Culture in the nineteenth century: much maligned for long, recognized as vibrant, now

Till the 1970s, the culture of the Netherlands during the nineteenth century usually was described as complacent, provincial and unoriginal. Nowadays people realize that there were many new, interesting developments, often characterised by a decided originality.

Painting: the 'School of The Hague' and Vincent van Gogh

After the flourishing of history painting at the beginning of the nineteenth century, the pictorial arts in the Netherlands became more academic: inspiration seemed to be derived solely from traditional themes. But during the second half of the century, a number of artists specializing in marine and landscape painting began to produce work that resembled and, it has to be said, even preceded the work of the School of Barbizon and the Impressionists in France. From the 1870s, a number of artists settled in or around The Hague were termed the 'School of The Hague'. Such men as Johan Weissenbruch and the internationally successful Anton Mauve belonged to this 'school'. Important work was being made, too, by the brothers Jacob and Willem Maris. A third brother, Matthijs, produced paintings akin to the Symbolists, a European movement which flourished briefly at the end of the nineteenth century. George Breitner painted in true Impressionist vein. His street scenes of Amsterdam are particularly expressive.

This, by and large surprisingly vital artistic climate, that gave opportunities to many, was the context within which the genius of Vincent van Gogh (1853-1890) could unfold. He, surely the best-known Dutch artist since Rembrandt, began working in Drenthe and Brabant, painting rural scenes that, sometimes, stressed the desperate conditions of the farming population, as shown in his famous 'Potato Eaters'. Admittedly, he created his most famous paintings after he had moved to France, where the bright light of the Provence never ceased to inspire him.

Vincent van Gogh
(1853-1890),
self-portrait (1887)
Kröller-Müller Museum

The early work of Piet Mondriaan has to be situated in this context as well. Showing Impressionist tendencies first, he developed along ever more Expressionist lines towards an almost absolute abstraction that has made him one of the major representatives of European Modernist painting.

Architecture: Cuypers and Berlage

After the 1850s, the restrained neo-classicism that had been fashionable for many decades was replaced by neo-Gothic architecture, mainly prompted by Roman Catholic emancipation. The major representative of this movement was the architect Pierre Cuypers, who restored and designed numerous Catholic churches all over the country. He also built the Amsterdam Central Station and the Rijksmuseum. This proved that emancipation really was making progress: even such 'national' monuments were given a neo-Gothic, and hence to many 'Catholic', appearance, despite the fact that Cuypers' critics, including King William III, did not hesitate to denounce the very aspect of these public and, hence prestigious buildings as not being 'national'.

Meanwhile, many architects rejected what they felt to be a return to decoration for its own sake and to the traditional ideas inherent in neo-Gothic building. Yet, precisely the tradition of craftsmanship that went with neo-Gothic architecture and interior decoration became a fertile soil from which grew the initiatives of new architects who truly innovated Dutch ar-

The entrance front of the Amsterdam Exchange, designed by H.P. Berlage

The 'Rijksmuseum' at Amsterdam, designed by P. Cuypers. It was inaugurated in 1885 and entirely restored between 2004 and 2013

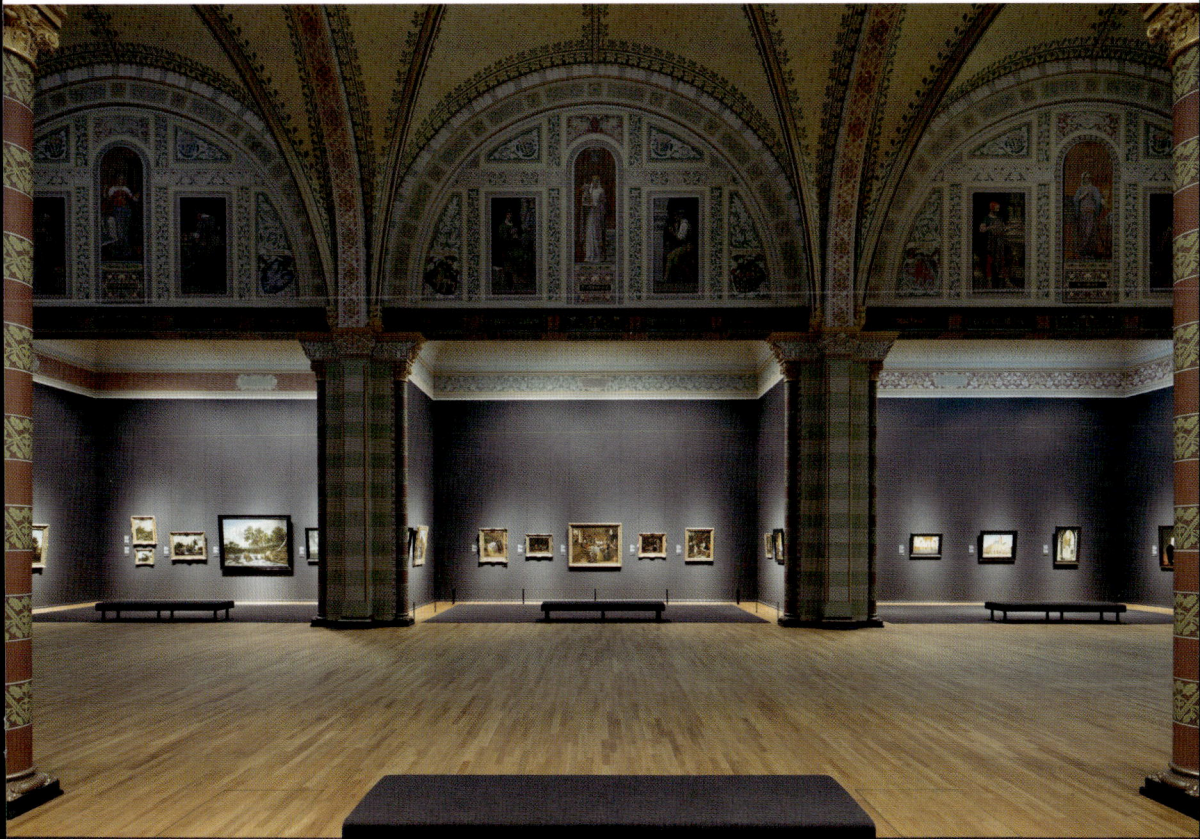

chitecture. Hendrik Berlage was one such innovator. His new Amsterdam Exchange, and the castle of St. Hubert on the Hoge Veluwe-estate of the art-collecting Kröller-Müller family reflected his conviction that the interior structure of a building should be visible in its outward appearance, not glossed over with unnecessary decoration.

Literature and music:
the 'Men of the Eighties' and the Socialists

As Dutch society became ever more industrialized, many people felt the need to escape from the anonymous, collectivist atmosphere that increasingly seemed to pervade life. That need was reflected not only in Impressionist painting but also in essayistic and creative literature.

Two famous periodicals show the spirit of late nineteenth-century Dutch culture: *De Gids* and *De Nieuwe Gids*. They were, broadly speaking, 'literary' reviews that both documented and, often, instigated new trends in Dutch

Louis Couperus (1863–1923), the most versatile of late 19th-century Dutch novelists

culture, also by introducing new ideas from abroad - mainly France and Germany.

Meanwhile, many younger authors rebelled against what they disparagingly termed the 'parson's poetry' of the mid-nineteenth century. The literary movement of the 'Men of the Eighties', that included (mostly male) writers and poets such as Jacques Perk and Willem Kloos, expressed an individualistic awareness of life, often resulting in a romantic, Impressionist glorification of nature. At the same time other authors decided to use poetry and literary prose precisely to highlight the problems of the new, industrial society, thus to attract attention to the (negative) conditions of modernity. Herman Gorter and Henriëtte Roland Holst were among those who expressed their mostly Socialist views in poetry. Among the novelists, the dandy-like, Fin-de-Siècle figure of Louis Couperus stands out. Had he written in English, French or German, he surely would have been one of Europe's major writers, with such powerful works as 'The Mountain of Light', evoking late-antique Rome, 'Of Old People the Things that Pass', set in the elite world of The Hague to which he himself belonged, and 'The Silent Force', that described the strange relationship between the Dutch colonists and the to them almost mystic Malay world of Java, also part of his own background.

Dutch music, that had not produced any great composer since Sweelinck, now flourished with the works of such men as Johannes van Bree, whose third symphony typically celebrated 'the fatherland', and Johannes Verhulst, who in his many songs used Dutch lyrics instead of the ubiquitous German poetry. They were followed by the one truly great Dutch composer of the past two centuries, Alphons Diepenbrock (1862-1921). A cultural critic as well, he wanted to reinstate music to its proper place in society and culture, searching for a synthesis between ancient Netherlandic musical forms, the new ideas put forward by Richard Wagner in Germany during the 1860s and 1870s, and the aesthetic of modern French composers like Claude Debussy who worked around the turn of the century. In doing so, Diepenbrock achieved an idiom quite his own, that only recently has been given the recognition it so obviously deserves.

Alphons Diepenbrock (1862–1921), perhaps the first Dutch 20th-century composer of international stature

Obviously, no society ever changes between specific dates, but it is safe to state that the first phase of Dutch industrialization was completed during the last decades of the nineteenth century. In the following years, the Netherlands became one of the most highly industrialized countries in the world, despite a lapse during the Great Depression in the nineteen-twenties and -thirties.

The need for neutrality

Already in the decade before the First World War actually broke out, the threat of war could be felt all over Europe. The Netherlands, too, took steps to defend itself in case of need, and laws were passed in 1912 and 1913 to bring the army up to standard. However, the very traditional wish to remain neutral, which had become something of a national obsession as early as the eighteenth century, prevailed. General mobilization was ordered in August 1914, but this was only in order to prepare for a possible infringement of Dutch neutrality by imperial Germany.

The Depression during the Thirties'

The economic depression that occurred after the First World War, reached its crisis in the period after 1929. The long-prevailing Liberal view that government should not intervene in economic affairs now clearly had become untenable. A growing consciousness of social problems also demanded measures other than those that promoted prosperity, only. Working hours had been cut in 1922, already. During the Depression, the state provided relief to the unemployed, guaranteeing them a minimum income, however small. When, in 1933, unemployment was exceptionally high, the Ministry of Social Affairs was established.

Unemployment peaked in 1935 with over 30% of the labour force on the dole. The Socialists then put forward their so-called 'Plan for Labour', as they strongly rejected Liberal ideas on factory management. It advocated substantial government investment and a truly planned economy. By devaluating the guilder, the government succeeded in cutting unemployment figures slightly, but by 1939 there still were 300,000 people jobless. Not surprisingly, during these difficult decades many people decided to leave their home country. For most emigrants, the United States, which already had received so many Dutchmen, remained their favourite destination.

Poster announcing the 'Exhibition for Peace and the League of Nations' in The Hague, 1930

Government policy during the Depression

The man who, as prime minister, left his mark on government policy in these years of crisis was Hendrik Colijn (1869-1944): he held office five times between 1925 and 1939. He obstinately worked to maintain the gold standard, looking upon the devaluation of the guilder as a moral and economic defeat. Though many disagreed with him, in the elections of 1937 he still won a great victory with his staunchly Calvinist, Anti-Revolutionary Party. Feeling the need for a strong leader, many non-Protestant

voters, too, wanted Colijn to govern again, which enabled him to form his fourth cabinet.

The main remedy Colijn had in mind to combat the Depression was to enforce drastic budget cuts. Obviously, this view clashed with the Socialist 'Plan for Labour'. While Colijn did not increase government expenditure, he did attempt to bring down unemployment figures by job-creation schemes. The major project was the reclamation of the Zuiderzee. As indicated, proposals to drain it had already been put forward in the nineteenth century, but had been rejected. In 1892, the plan of Cornelis Lely (1854-1929) was approved.

However, this gigantic scheme was not executed until 1918, when Lely himself had been appointed Minister of Public Works and his bill for the partial reclamation of this vast inner sea was passed. Once the Wieringermeer-polder had been drained in 1930, the Zuiderzee was permanently closed off towards the open North Sea by the IJsselmeer Dam, completed in 1933. Reclamation of the Northeast-polder was already in progress, but due to the lack of funds work was stopped in the second half of the thirties.

Socialist demonstration in The Hague, in 1932

Multinationals

Despite widespread social misery, there were favourable economic developments. The rich sources of raw materials in the Dutch East Indies, and later the strong position of Dutch trade and industry on the international market combined to promote the establishment and growth of a number of companies which soon became multinationals - some of them due to the initiatives of individual entrepreneurs. Among these were the Steenkolen HandelsVereniging (SHV) - originally dealing in coal but soon diversifying - and the Royal Dutch Petroleum Company, which later merged with the English Shell, as well as, of course, during

the nineteen-twenties and -thirties, the Philips electronics concern. Innovating such traditional Dutch businesses as, for example, dredging and other forms of water management, a few companies gained an international position in this field as well.

Pacifism and Fascism in the Netherlands between the World Wars

Between the two World Wars, the Netherlands proved a loyal member of the recently formed League of Nations, the predecessor of the United Nations. Indeed, pacifist ideas once more dominated the policy of most Dutch political parties. Pacifism even led to constitutional revision in 1922, when it was ruled that war could only be declared with the approval of the States-General.

Until a few years before the Second World War, most parties did not give up their pacifist stance. By that time, however, their faith in a peaceful solution of world conflicts had been badly shaken both by changes in international relations and by developments at home.

Already in the early nineteen-twenties, in the Netherlands, as in the rest of Europe, a number of sometimes extremely nationalistic organizations

The Philips Competence Centre at Eindhoven, symbol of the techno-logical contributions made by this Dutch multinational

had been founded. Their members doubted whether parliamentary democ-racy could survive, regarded pacifism as useless and even dangerous, and generally demanded that power be given to a strong leader, who would revive the nation and solve all its current problems. Soon, one of these organizations, the National-Socialist Movement (N.S.B.) joined the political arena proper. In the 1935 elections, the N.S.B. even succeeded in winning almost 8% of the votes. At that time, the party was not particularly pro-Ger-man or anti-Jewish, yet. This only changed in later years when it drifted in-creasingly into the German camp. Their spectacular 1935-election victory can be explained from the fact that in these years the Dutch economy was at its lowest ebb; this caused many people to feel that a strong man - such as many people thought was in power in Germany - was indeed needed to reorganize politics and the economy and work a way out of the existing misery. Consequently, various anti-Fascist movements arose, fully aware of the danger of these anti-democratic tendencies. This helped reinstate trust in Dutch democracy, and the N.S.B. was defeated in the elections of 1937, after which its numbers dwindled rapidly.

By that time, the gravity of the international situation was clear. Yet even in 1939, the almost innate Dutch tendency to remain neutral, coupled to principled pacifism, led many to believe that the Netherlands should avoid engaging in the war that was so obviously approaching. In August, the King of the Belgians and Queen Wilhelmina, who, of course, stemmed from a German family herself and had married a German prince, offered to mediate between Germany and the other European states. Nevertheless, general mobilization was called for in the same month. It was evident that this time the Netherlands would not be able to maintain its neutrality.

The iconic chair designed c. 1920 by G. Rietveld

The modernist town hall of Hilversum designed by W. Dudok, c. 1925

A new movement in the visual arts: 'The Style'

During the first decades of the twentieth century, the Netherlands did participate in the general renewal of cultural life in Europe. Many writers and poets, painters and architects were influenced by the obvious need to rethink old values. The disaster that had been the First World War, also morally, had taught them that an uncritical continuation of the much-vaunted European tradition would be dangerous.

Among the many developments in the arts, there was one that gained international interest. It was named after a journal which first appeared in 1917, called 'The Style'. Its founders represented various art forms. For instance, Theo van Doesburg and Piet Mondriaan were painters, while J.J.P. Oud was an architect. The keynote of 'The Style' was to strip art of every unnecessary detail, following the idea of 'function over form'. In architecture, this meant that buildings stressed their structure and avoided any ornamentation. Among the most striking and beautiful examples of the 'The Style'-movement are the Hilversum town hall, by Willem Dudok, and the Schröder House in Utrecht, a private dwelling designed by Gerrit Rietveld in 1924 as a three-dimensional plaything of flat planes and strong primary colours; it now is open to the public.

Literature

The same moralism that pervaded the visual arts also was found in literature. Writers such as Menno Ter Braak, Hendrik Marsman, Eduard Du Perron and Jan Jacob Slauerhoff wanted to uphold and pass on the essence and the best of the Dutch literary tradition by stripping it of false ornament and sentiment. Their popular appeal, though, was limited. The work of Ferdinand Bordewijk, especially his tersely written novels *Blokken* and *Bint*, gained a wider readership and still enjoy popularity today. The poets J.C. Bloem and Martinus Nijhoff were less controversial and polemic. Since all of them felt this was a time for reflection as well as action, their works showed a new vitality that even after so many years remains recognisable.

Music

In creative composition, Dutch musicians on the whole did not contribute works of international standing, though Willem Pijper, who wrote both chamber music and opera, of late has gained a deserved recognition, while Willem Andriessen certainly had a dedicated following even in his own time.

This lack of truly great composers may surprise in view of the fact that in these very years the Amsterdam Concertgebouw Orchestra won increasing fame, both at home and abroad, especially through its performances of modern music. Since 1920, its chief conductor, Willem Mengelberg, had earned an international reputation. He laid the foundation for the orchestra's renown as the ideal performers of the music not only of such contemporary Dutch composers as Hendrik Andriessen and Willem Pijper, but also of foreign masters such as Gustav Mahler, who was his personal friend, and Richard Strauss.

Three novels (1931–1934) by the famous modernist author F. Bordewijk

The mass media

During the first decades of the twentieth century, the new mass media - film, radio and the gramophone - made their entry in the Netherlands as well. They soon revolutionized Dutch social life, allowing a far greater group of people to participate in all sorts of culture.

Already in the nineteen-thirties, most families owned a wireless set. They listened to (world) news bulletins, sports commentaries and to music, both popular and classical, that formerly was beyond the means of most; they also listened to the radio plays, which soon became highly popular.

The fact that each of the many broadcasting corporations that now were founded represented a specific religious denomination or ideology again shows the extent to which the 'pillarization' of Dutch society, its division in groups with their own religious identity, pervaded cultural life in all its respects. Three of the corporations still operating today have been active since 1925.

Science

The leading position of the Netherlands as an industrial nation also was reflected in its marked progress in the sciences and in engineering. In the first decades of the twentieth century, the laboratories of the universities of Leiden and Amsterdam produced a number of Nobel Prize winners. In mathematics, physics and astronomy, H. Kamerlingh Onnes, J.C. Kapteyn, H. Lorentz and J.H. Van der Waals had a worldwide reputation.

27 Society and politics during the Second World War

The German occupation: 1940-945

On May, the 10th, 1940, German troops invaded the Netherlands. This marked the end of a period of peace which had lasted for over a century. For after all, the country had managed to stay out of international conflicts since the struggle with Belgium in 1839 had ended with its separation from the Dutch kingdom. Now, neutrality could no longer be maintained.

After several days of fighting it was obvious that the poorly-equipped Dutch army was no match for the superior strength of the Germans. On May, 13, Queen Wilhelmina and her cabinet ministers left for England unhindered, after foiling German plans to take them prisoner. Though many accepted this as a wise move, others felt the monarch should have stayed with her subjects. A catastrophic and devastating bombardment of Rotterdam and Middelburg followed, leaving the towns almost totally destroyed. When the Germans threatened to attack other cities if resistance continued, the Dutch army command was forced to capitulate on May, the 15th.

In May 1940, German bombers razed the inner city of Rotterdam

The persecution and deportation of the Jews

Already on May, 29, Arthur Seyss-Inquart took up position as the German Reich's commissioner for the Netherlands. It soon appeared the anti-Semitic policies pursued by the German government at home would also be conducted abroad, inevitably affecting the considerable Jewish population of the Netherlands, which had been part of Dutch society for several centuries. In October 1940, all civil servants had to produce a declaration of 'Aryan origin', showing they had no Jewish blood. The majority of the population did not yet realize the extent of German anti-Semitism, causing many such declarations to be signed. However, it has to be admitted that the Dutch, as a society and culture, were not entirely free of anti-Semitic feelings themselves.

The Jewish quarter of Amsterdam, the main street renamed 'Judenstrasse'/Jew Street by the German authorities
Foto J. Rotgans, GAA

Any hopes that the Jews in this country would not be persecuted and deported were dashed in July 1942. Then, the first groups of Jewish Dutchmen were transported to the extermination camps in Germany and Poland, under the pretext of being given employment, there. In little more than a year's time, some 100,000 Jews were taken away and subsequently murdered. Thus, almost the entire Jewish population of the Netherlands was wiped out. Only a few escaped deportation by going into hiding with those Dutch

Jewish Dutchmen being deported to the German extermination camps

The 'National Monument' on Dam Square, Amsterdam, designed by J. Radecker and J.J.P. Oud to com-memorate the war and the liberation

people willing to help them - including, of course, the Frank-family, whose daughter Anne kept a diary that after the war would expose the horror of what had happened to its millions of readers.

Meanwhile, resistance organizations had been formed at an early stage. During the war, they were to play an important part in espionage activities and in helping those who, like the Jews, soon realized they had to hide. Above all they helped to keep up the morale of the Dutch people, the majority of whom, unlike the members of the National-Socialist Movement, did not collaborate with the Germans. From London, Queen Wilhelmina made her own contribution by encouraging her subjects in her clandestinely received broadcasts via Radio Orange. As a result, the royal family became a symbol of freedom.

The liberation of the Netherlands: 1944 and 1945

On June, the 6th, 1944, the Allied armies - including Dutch units assembled abroad - landed in Normandy. When news of the invasion reached the Netherlands, it was followed by 'Mad Tuesday', the 5th of September. It was started by a rumour that parts of the country had already been liberated by allied soldiers; the rumour was so strong that German troops and numerous National Socialists hastily left for the eastern frontier.

But yet another winter passed before the whole of the Netherlands was freed, a winter of famine during which many died and that became a traumatic experience for those who managed to live through it. All means of transport had been requisitioned by the Germans; distribution

of food, especially in the west of the country, now came to a virtual standstill. The result were severe shortages everywhere. When part of the Netherlands was actually liberated on April, the 29th, 1945, the first of a series of food parcels was dropped by Allied airplanes, to the immense relief of the starving population.

For the Netherlands, the war formally ended on May, the 5th, 1945, when the Germans signed the capitulation in the presence of Prince Bernhard, the ambitious husband of Crown Princess Juliana. Born a German himself, and in his youth a member of the various National-Socialist organizations, in September 1944 he had assumed command of the so-called 'Domestic Force', though he had no military experience at all. The force was an umbrella organization for the various resistance groups, if only because by now these often fought amongst themselves, having different ideas of how to organize public life after the war. The return of the royal family, i.e. the Queen, Wilhelmina, her only child, the heir to the throne Juliana, and her three granddaughters Beatrix, Irene and Margriet, was a sign to all that the war was really over.

Queen Wilhelmina and her only child, Princess Juliana, personified the House of Orange after their return from exile in Britain and Canada

Clearing the rubble and starting again: new politics and new parties

During the first post-war years, the succeeding governments could accomplish little more than clearing the rubble, to begin with quite literally. Still, during the war ideas had been born and discussed in various socio-political circles that now were put into practice, in the hope of altering the structure of Dutch society to finally solve some of the worst pre-war problems, both social and economic. Indeed, a number of pre-war situations did not recur. For example, council housing ensured that people with a low income could now move into homes with modern conveniences. Of course this did not materialize immediately; indeed, the housing shortage continued for a very long time.

Some of the pre-war political parties were not revived. New parties were founded, however, though a few still based their ideas on the old ideals of Liberalism and Socialism but adapted them to the realities of post-war life. These included the Labour Party'' (PVDA), formed in 1946, the Liberal 'People's Party for Freedom and Democracy' (VVD), formed in 1948, and the 'Catholic People's Party' (KVP), also formed after the war. Two pre-war parties that did return were the ones based on Protestant principles: the 'Christian Historical Union' and the 'Anti-Revolutionary Party'. In 1976, these two merged with the KVP to form the present 'Christian Democratic Appeal' (CDA).

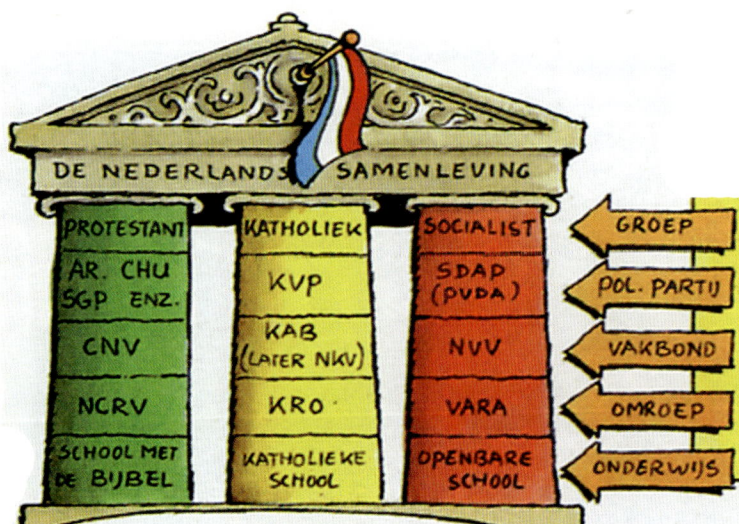

The 'pillars' that, even after the Second World War, continued to uphold Dutch society and politics

International co-operation and integration

As a small country that had suffered greatly from the war between the European states, the Netherlands were eager indeed to join those international organizations that strove to work for a situation in which such a disaster would not happen again. From its start in 1945, the Netherlands were a member of the United Nations. They also joined the NATO from the first. Deeply grateful to the Americans for their wartime effort, and for the Marshall Plan that had contributed to the economic rebuilding of Europe, the Dutch, for decades, continued to feel that the United States were the one power that would safeguard the interests of Europe, especially since the Cold War threat of the 1950's seemed to jeopardize the newly-won freedom again.

Moreover, in 1947 already, a customs' union was formed with Belgium and Luxembourg, which was consolidated in the so-called Benelux in 1948. This, of course, has been one of the many steps that eventually resulted in the establishment of the European Community. Till the 1990's, it has had the support of many Dutchmen, maybe not because they actually wished to create pan-European unity but in the hope that their ideals regarding their own society would be upheld and strengthened, especially by the advantages of European economic and political co-operation.

The Dutch East Indies declares its independence:
Indonesia is born

After the war, the colonies, which already had been renamed 'overseas territories' in a 1922-constitutional reform, became (semi-)independent. In the case of the Dutch East Indies, this was preceded by an unsuccessful Dutch military campaign to yet retain some power over the archipelago. For immediately following the capitulation of Japan, which had occupied the Dutch East Indies for almost four of the war years, indigenous political groups had declared the independence of 'Indonesia'. The Dutch government then considered granting independence to 'the United States of Indonesia', hoping to yet keep it as part of the Dutch kingdom. In 1946,

The transfer of Dutch sovereignty over 'the Dutch East Indies' to the new Indonesian Republic in 1949
Anefo

an agreement to this effect was signed between the Netherlands and the Republic of Indonesia at Lingadjati. The new Republic, which dominated the islands of Sumatra and Java, wanted to extend its power to the other parts of the archipelago, which for a number of reasons did not welcome this development. In the ensuing confusion, in 1947 the first, sometimes bloody 'police actions' were carried out by the Dutch government, when Dutch troops, as soon appeared: unsuccessfully, tried to protect the interests of these other regions, as well as the hope that the vision of a 'united kingdom' could yet be realized. After a second campaign in 1949, a round-table conference was held at The Hague, partly following international pressure. On December 27 of that year, sovereignty was transferred and the Republic of Indonesia was given the freedom to try and gain command of the entire archipelago.

The Charter of the Kingdom is granted to the colonies in the West

Already in 1948, a round-table conference had been convened to discuss the future relationship between the Netherlands, Surinam and the Dutch Antilles. Another followed and, after a third one, in 1954, the Charter of the Kingdom was established, granting these overseas territories in the West Indies far-reaching independence. Surinam became completely autonomous in 1975. Aruba, Curacao and St. Maarten opted for independence, but within the kingdom. In 2010, the islands of Bonaire, Saba and St. Eustabius decided to become district councils within the kingdom.

Young Queen Wilhelmina (1880–1962). She ruled from 1898 till 1948

The House of Orange

To Queen Wilhelmina, the post-war period in the Netherlands was a disappointment. During the war she had developed some quite explicit notions about a strongly coherent and, indeed, strongly ruled society. But the highly varied and to her confusing reality of politics in the years following the war did not live up to her expectations. In 1948, after having celebrated her fiftieth anniversary on the throne, she abdicated in favour of her only child, Juliana.

In the twenty-first century, Dutch sovereignty still is embodied in a member of the House of Orange. In 1980, Queen Juliana in her turn abdicated in favour of her eldest daughter, Queen Beatrix who, till she herself abdicated in 2013, has symbolized the unity of the people of the Netherlands in her own, much respected way.

Meanwhile, as in most contemporary monarchies, in recent years the Dutch royal family, too, has been hampered by the increased attention of especially the mass media, who demand both the continued mystique of royalty and, at the same time but incompatible with it, its openness and accommodation to the demands of a modern popular culture.

Thus, when in the 1950's the media revealed Queen Juliana, who during her Canadian exile had strongly helped to support the Dutch war effort, now was ethically and perhaps also politically influenced by the heavily pacifist ideas of a few close advisers, a crisis loomed. Again, when, in the 1970's, her husband, Prince Bernhard, was accused of having taken bribes during his promotional activities for Dutch industry, the monarchy only narrowly escaped a second crisis. The choice of Beatrix, while still crown princess, to take as her husband a German nobleman, provoked bitter resentment amongst those who remembered the misery of the war, though, in the following decades, most Dutchmen came to deeply respect Prince Claus as, indeed, a model prince, who combined compassion with a great and intelligent interest in Dutch and world affairs. When their eldest son Prince Willem-Alexander decided to marry a young lady from Argentina, who happened to be the daughter of a man who had been part of the country's former military government, Parliament asked for a formal enquiry before giving its consent. Indeed, by the twenty-first century the royal children and grandchildren, so much more open to public scrutiny than any of their forebears, face the problem of having to live a life that if it shows any 'scandal' will elicit much public criticism. However, despite the slow but perhaps inevitable erosion of the symbolic function of the monarchy, few Dutchmen as yet voice any strong preference for a republican constitution.

Queen Juliana (1909–2004).
She ruled from 1948 till 1980

Queen Beatrix (1938–).
She ruled from 1980 till 2013

Infrastructural projects – and the Delta Plan realized

During the second part of the twentieth century, a great deal of work has been done in civil engineering. Many motorways have been built, to accommodate a growing number of cars. Indeed, people have complained that in a country so small, not all of the still available countryside should be tarred over to enable everyone to decide on his own movements rather than accept what public transport has to offer. Admittedly, provisions in that sector often fail to be up to the mark.

Meanwhile, the Zuiderzee-project was strengthened with the reclamation of eastern and southern Flevoland. The debate concerning the reclamation of the western part known as Markerwaard is still going on, since the need to add more arable land to the country is debated.

An even greater project, realized over the past decades, was the Delta Plan, designed following a disastrous storm which flooded the islands of Zeeland in 1953, at the cost of 1835 lives. The project aims to protect the low-lying areas of the South-West Netherlands. It was started in 1957, when all the Zeeland sea inlets were sealed off. The storm barrier in the Eastern Scheldt was brought into operation by Queen Beatrix in 1986. By then, this gigantic feat of engineering had taken almost thirty years to complete. Together with the Zuider Zee-project, it has strengthened the world-wide reputation of the Dutch in this field. However, at the beginning

The Easter Scheldt Barrier is part of the great Delta project to safeguard the western provinces of The Netherlands against the North Sea

King William–Alexander (1967–), pledging his allegiance to the Dutch constitution on 30 April 2013

New factories estab-
lished on the artificial
plain bordering the
mouth of the River
Maas near Rotterdam

of the twenty-first century, concerns are being voiced over the consequences of climate change and the subsequent rising of the sea level. Under the
worst scenario, the present Dutch dykes might fail to keep the sea from
once more claiming the better part of the country's western provinces;
moreover, the great rivers, too, now endanger the surrounding low-lying
lands with inundation. Thus, not only another major engineering feat will
be needed, but also a financial effort that may well exceed anything envisaged thus far.

Economic boom and economic recession: legislation for social welfare and increasing social problems

After the war, many people were unable or unwilling to wait for the
economy to recover. Once more, they decided to emigrate. At the beginning of the 1950's, hundreds of thousands left the country. This time their
major destinations were Australia, Canada and New Zealand. However, in
the same period a wave of immigrants started arriving from the Dutch East
Indies: Dutchmen who had lived there, sometimes for generations, but
also people from the Moluccas, unhappy with the new political situation in
Indonesia. In the following decades, a steady stream of hundreds of thousands started arriving from Surinam and the Antilles as well.

Meanwhile, there was work to be done in the Netherlands if only because the Dutch, like other people all over western Europe, were stimulated by the American Marshall Plan, that provided a major economic and
financial incentive. Food rationing was lifted in 1949 and during several
rounds of wage increases, each time amounting to some 5%, the standard
of living rose through increased spending power and increased economic
growth. This policy, coupled with fresh investments, expanding industries
and growing exports, did indeed help boost the economy from the end of
the 1950's onwards. However, as a result the Dutch economy, while definitely prospering, also became far more sensitive to global fluctuations,

Dr. Willem Drees (1886–
1988), the 'father of
the Dutch Welfare
State'

which has proved a problem ever since.

Soon, the growing prosperity was being translated into a national social and, even, welfare policy. It is indelibly stamped by the efforts of one of the major post-war politicians, Dr. Willem Drees (1886-1988). As Minister of Social Affairs in the first two post-war cabinets, he succeeded in launching special legislation to improve the lot of the old-age pensioners. Between 1948 and 1958, he also was prime minister, heading four coalition governments that gathered together all the major parties. The Dutch social security system that, since then, has formed the basis of the much-admired and much-maligned Dutch 'welfare state', has its roots in this period. However, the system was not really put to the test, if only because the 1950's were followed by two decades of great affluence, the 1960's and the 1970's. Indeed, these were the very years all kinds of social legislation were enacted that, while addressing the needs of many groups, also raised their expectations of state intervention to a level that, as even then some pessimists predicted, would be unsustainable if the economy declined again.

In the 1960's, to keep prosperity growing while unemployment figures were falling, it was considered necessary to recruit immigrant labour from Italy, Greece and Spain and later also from Morocco and Turkey. While the first generation of these immigrant labourers envisaged returning home after a stint of profitable work in the Netherlands, many soon decided it was in their own interest to settle here permanently. At home, unemployment still prevailed, while in their adoptive country, even if job opportunities fell, they might still expect to live well on social benefits. As government allowed the immigrants to also bring over their families, the Netherlands soon had a growing population with a predominantly Islamic rather than Christian culture and religion.

One of the results was that, combined with steady immigration from Surinam and the Antilles, the Netherlands soon turned into a multiracial and, indeed, a veritable multicultural society. In the 1970's and 1980's, politicians decided it would reflect Dutch tradition as well as the needs of contemporary society to allow and indeed financially enable all minority groups to uphold their own cultural values. In retrospect, it is easy to see that far too little stress was placed on the necessity to at least demand of all newcomers that they adopted the basic values of Dutch society and culture, to begin with the language, rather than granting people citizenship without pre-set proper conditions.

When economic decline did set in during the 1980's and continued after the short boom of the 1990's, the social security system was really put to the test. Its partial but continuing demolition since then - which has specifically and negatively affected the care of the elderly - has led to increased social and political debate and, even, tension. During the period of unheard-of affluence between 1960 and 1974 people, especially the young, had enthusiastically embraced all kind of new ideas, as well as discussing new political and cultural issues. In recent years, however, their efforts once more concentrate on ordering their lives and futures as materially - perhaps even as materialistically - comfortable as possible. With the em-

In the 1960s and 1970s, an increasingly educated and prosperous middle class turned its attention to big political issues, such as the spread of nuclear weapons and racism

ployment situation fluctuating since the 1980's, and social services being less generous, the average Dutch person is intent on finding and holding on to a job. This leaves little time for outspoken social or cultural criticism.

The changing situation also was reflected in foreign policy that, during the first decades following the war, had been dominated by the need to maintain peace. In the 1960's and 1970's, many Dutchmen abhorred the arms' race between Western and Eastern Europe, and huge protest demonstrations were organized to express their revulsion against the use of nuclear weapons. Particularly among Leftists, this pacifist attitude sometimes became violently anti-American. However, since the disarmament talks between Russia and America and especially since the fall of Communism in Eastern Europe in 1989 and 1990, political awareness has been far less obvious.

During the last decades of the twentieth century, the general public's involvement in the serious problems facing society seems to have grown less intense, too, perhaps due to their concern over individual economic well-being. However, in the early years of the twenty-first century, a politician arose who at least seemingly voiced the opinions of many Dutchmen normally politically silent. Flamboyantly gay, Pim Fortuyn (1948-2002) articulated his concerns over a range of issues confronting Dutch society: the lack of integration of the Islamic part of the population, by now rising to ca 1 million on a total of some 16 million people; the ineffectiveness of the public health service; the problems facing education; the money spent on cultural and societal 'fashions' which, he argued, were affordable no longer, et cetera. While admitting that the Netherlands still were a great country, he yet admonished the electorate to be aware of the dangers threatening it. As he was murdered in 2002 - by an environmental activist - he never had a chance to prove whether he could have delivered on his many promises. Of course, the murder itself was a great shock to the Dutch who, perhaps over-complacently, had thought no such thing would ever happen in a society as tolerant as theirs.

Cultural life after 1960

Education in the Netherlands has been entirely re-organized since the war, starting with the 'Mammoth Act' regulating secondary schools that was passed in 1963 and implemented in 1968. This legislation was meant to promote the mobility of one level of schooling to another, especially for the benefit of those social groups who traditionally were not readily admitted to higher education. The Primary Education Act implemented in 1985 did away with the distinction between the infant and primary schools, bringing the start of formal education down to the age of 5. The reorganization of higher education in the 1980's led to cuts in the length of university studies, and to mergers between the various forms of vocational training.

The underlying question whether education is the most efficient instrument to effectuate social change, through providing equality of opportu-

nities, still remains unanswered, if only because, obviously, employment or non-employment will greatly affect people's subsequent position in life. However, since the early 1990's, the, to many inexplicable but constant demand for educational change voiced by politicians, government officials and social theorists alike has led to serious dissatisfaction in the educational field itself. There, or so people feel, time that should be spent on the learning process, and on slowly implementing only the most necessary of changes is being wasted on an ever growing bureaucracy that seems to have become an aim in itself, besides absorbing an inordinate amount of the educational budget.

One of the most creative post-war artistic movements in the Netherlands - the abstract art produced by members of the Cobra-group - became internationally famous, especially through the work of Karel Appel (1921-2006). A younger generation of Dutch painters yet has to make its mark. Indeed, many feel that modern art in the Netherlands, as all over Europe, perhaps has become too fashion-conscious, stimulating people to work for instant commercial success rather than for a durable reputation or a challenge to existing ideas.

In literature, the 'Men of the Fifties' included Lucebert and Remco Campert, both of whom wrote experimental poetry. The prose writer

Gerard van 't Reve (1923-2006) also broke with tradition. He established his fame with the novel 'The Evenings', that was the perfect description of life immediately following the war, of the sober years of the Reconstruction Period. It brilliantly evoked both the prevailing restrictions people had to live with and the glimmers of hope for change, for a more exciting life they held on to.

Indeed, after the Second World War there was a general longing for a breakthrough to more freedom of expression in the various fields of culture, unhampered by a tradition that according to many had ended in disaster. Was not this the lesson World War II had taught? These feelings seem reminiscent of the mood in the period after World War I.

However, as in many western countries, during the latter decades of the twentieth century Dutch literary critics, too, felt literary production was a bit lacklustre, showing little vigour. Perhaps, however, we need a longer perspective to be able to judge whether this view has not been, after all, too pessimistic.

Dutch musical culture is, as everywhere, definitely divided between a small 'serious', and a huge 'popular' market. Nevertheless, such composers as Louis Andriessen and Peter Schat, to name but two, have gained an

The combined Town Hall/ Music Theatre of Amsterdam designed by W. Holzbauer and C. Dam, opened 1986/1987

international reputation while the Dutch National Opera, in its new house in Amsterdam, is widely acclaimed as a place where new ideas are being tried to keep alive an old genre. Popular music obviously follows international trends though in recent years groups working to create a Dutch sound - and, indeed, using Dutch lyrics - have been successful. Yet, it is not the Dutch arts in the broadest sense that shape the image of Dutch society abroad. Rather, it is the idea that the Netherlands continue being unique in championing freedom of expression on a wide range of issues. Undeniably, since the Second World War, Dutch society has become liberal, tolerant in a sense it never was. Most visibly, this has demonstrated itself in greater freedom in the fields of sexual life and of the use of drugs. Consequently, many uninformed foreigners now allow an exaggerated vision of this aspect of Dutch life to colour their view of Dutch culture; rather deplorably, to many the 'red light district' in Amsterdam for a long time has taken precedence over the Rijksmuseum. Also, the heated, and internationally-mediated discussions over such questions as, first, the use of birth-control devices and, later, of the rights of gay people - the debate over the latter culminating in Parliament's decision that homosexual men and women were allowed to formally marry - have created an anything-goes image of Dutch society and culture that certainly does not reflect a reality that is both more complex and, indeed, moderate. Obviously, the on-going debate on the acceptance of euthanasia, often very partially and one-sidedly reported abroad as well, has done little to alter this image.

Basically, this freedom to discuss and, often, to change culture in the widest sense has become possible because during the 1950's and 1960's the barriers between the traditional socio-religious 'compartments' or 'pillars' were rapidly breaking down. It became increasingly obvious that culture and society could not be confined anymore within the traditional religious and ideological subgroups. The churches emptied, and the Churches - both Roman Catholic and Protestant - started losing their members. But the loss of tradition and of the socio-cultural framework that used to provide a sense of security, sometimes seems to make people long for old ideas and movements, which now are being eclectically recombined to provide new meanings, as can be seen in the great popularity of all sorts of 'New Age'-ideas and ideologies. Obviously, a new culture is taking shape, that may be 'global' while retaining a number of local, Dutch characteristics in its continued sense of controlled freedom.

However, with the economy less prosperous than in the 1960's and 1970's, and with the related problems of unemployment and the defective inclusion of cultural and religious minorities, the twenty-first century does present the people of the Netherlands with considerable challenges, even altering their traditionally tolerant culture and, also, their pro-European stance.

King Willem Alexander, Queen Maxima, former Queen Beatrix and, from left to right, Princess Alexia, Princess Amalia (heir to the throne), and Princess Ariane

30 april 2013

RVD

Conclusion

Obviously, one should not end a historical survey with predictions for the future. Yet it seems fitting to point out that, generally speaking, in the twenty-first century the Dutch, reviewing their past and pondering over their present, are struggling to regain a clearly defined idea of the identity that should shape their own culture and society and its role in Europe and the world.

The Netherlands always has been a small country, apt to boast of its greatness, economical, social, moral even. Won from the water, formerly one of the leading commercial powers in the world, it is still one of the world's most highly industrialized and prosperous societies. It also has endeavoured to attain and retain a high standard of social justice. The coming decades will reveal whether these achievements can stand the test of time.

In November, 2004, the well-known cinematographer Theo van Gogh was knifed to death by a young man of Islamic extraction. Unlike the murder of Fortuyn, that had no relationship whatsoever to problems of religion and multiculturalism, this crime originated in religious fanaticism - also because, shortly before, Van Gogh had premiered a film that was highly critical of traditional Islam as he understood it. The shock caused by this act of violence intensified public debate about the nature of Dutch society, indeed, about what it meant or should mean to be 'Dutch'.

The Netherlands long has been a small state that since the 1950s was prepared to relinquish some of the traditional elements of sovereignty and independence to promote and, indeed, retain welfare and wellbeing in a broader, European setting. In this respect, too, the next decades will show not only whether this policy bears fruit but also whether the Dutch will feel culturally confident enough to continue to do so. When, as all over Europe, the Dutch were called to vote on the draft for a European constitution, the negative result of the 2005-referendum surprised many politicians.

Indeed, people who have been studying the prevailing political-cultural climate note that, for the time being, the majority of the Dutch seem to favour a rather more national stance. In short, while the Netherlands always was a small nation that liked to think of itself as both tolerant and cosmopolitan, the coming decades will reveal whether this view still reflects reality. The outcome of the ongoing processes of adaptation and change, to altering European and global, but also to altering economic and social situations, will decide whether the Netherlands will remain a country, a state, a nation that rightly can continue to claim to be 'small among the great'.

Chronilogical outline

	Prehistory	**18th century**	**The Republic politically a second-rate power**
c. 10,000 B.C.	The last ice age		
c. 1900−750 B.C.	The bronze age	1747	Oranges hereditary stadhouders
c. 750 B.C.	The iron age		Patriots and Orangists
57 B.C.−A.D. 406	**Roman rule**	**1795−1806**	**The Batavian Republic**
until c. 650	Germanic society, Saxons, Frisians, Franks Conversion to Christianity	1806−1810	**The Kingdom of Holland,** King Louis Napoleon
		1810−1813	The French Period
c. 650−850	**The Carolingian Empire**		
800−814	Charlemagne	**1814−1830/39**	**The Kingdom of the United Netherlands**
c. 850−1000	The Norsemen	1814−1840	King William I
		1830	Establishment of the Belgian State
c. 1000	The development of territorial principalities Regional sovereignty	**1839**	**The Kingdom of the Netherlands**
		1840−1849	King William II
c. 1200	The towns set the tone in politics, economy and culture	1849−1890	King William III
		1890−1948	Queen Wilhelmina
		1948−1980	Queen Juliana
1350−1581	**Burgundian-Habsburg rule**	1980−2013	Queen Beatrix
	Centralization of power	2013−	King William-Alexander
	The Reformation	1840 and 1848	Constitutional revisions
1515−1555	Charles V		
1555−1581	Philip II	1840−1890	Towards an industrial society: phase I
1586−1648	**The 'Eighty Years' War': Rebellion against foreign rule**	1890−1940	Towards an industrial society: phase II
1576	The Pacification of Gent	1914−1945	Policy of neutrality. Pacifism
1579	The Union of Atrecht and the Union of Utrecht	1914−1918	World War I Economic crisis Fascism
1581	**The Act of Abjuration**	1940−1945	World War II
1581	Actual establishment of 'The Republic of the Seven United Provinces'	**1945−c. 1960**	**Reconstruction** International Co-operation
1648	The Peace of Munster: formal recognition of the Dutch Republic	c. 1960−c. 1980	Economic boom; the 'welfare state'
17th century	**The 'Dutch Golden Age'.** Voyages of discovery	c. 1980−	Further European integration Quest for an equilibrium in a social and multicultural society
1602 and 1621	Establishment of United East India Company and West India Company		

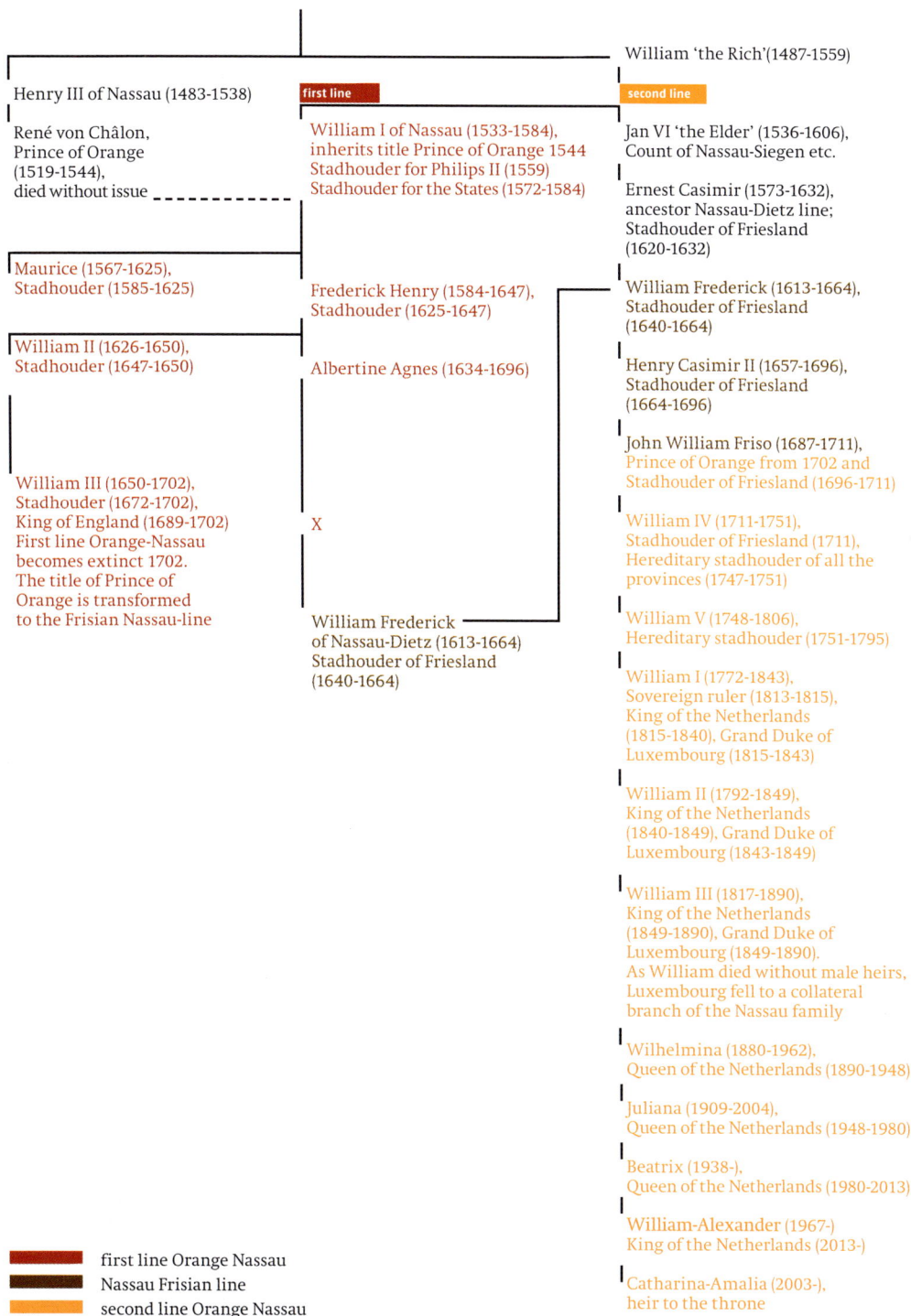

Simplified family tree of the House of Orange-Nassau

Jan V Count

William 'the Rich'(1487-1559)

Henry III of Nassau (1483-1538)

first line

second line

René von Châlon,
Prince of Orange
(1519-1544),
died without issue

William I of Nassau (1533-1584),
inherits title Prince of Orange 1544
Stadhouder for Philips II (1559)
Stadhouder for the States (1572-1584)

Jan VI 'the Elder' (1536-1606),
Count of Nassau-Siegen etc.

Ernest Casimir (1573-1632),
ancestor Nassau-Dietz line;
Stadhouder of Friesland
(1620-1632)

Maurice (1567-1625),
Stadhouder (1585-1625)

Frederick Henry (1584-1647),
Stadhouder (1625-1647)

William Frederick (1613-1664),
Stadhouder of Friesland
(1640-1664)

William II (1626-1650),
Stadhouder (1647-1650)

Albertine Agnes (1634-1696)

Henry Casimir II (1657-1696),
Stadhouder of Friesland
(1664-1696)

John William Friso (1687-1711),
Prince of Orange from 1702 and
Stadhouder of Friesland (1696-1711)

William III (1650-1702),
Stadhouder (1672-1702),
King of England (1689-1702)
First line Orange-Nassau
becomes extinct 1702.
The title of Prince of
Orange is transformed
to the Frisian Nassau-line

X

William IV (1711-1751),
Stadhouder of Friesland (1711),
Hereditary stadhouder of all the
provinces (1747-1751)

William Frederick
of Nassau-Dietz (1613-1664)
Stadhouder of Friesland
(1640-1664)

William V (1748-1806),
Hereditary stadhouder (1751-1795)

William I (1772-1843),
Sovereign ruler (1813-1815),
King of the Netherlands
(1815-1840), Grand Duke of
Luxembourg (1815-1843)

William II (1792-1849),
King of the Netherlands
(1840-1849), Grand Duke of
Luxembourg (1843-1849)

William III (1817-1890),
King of the Netherlands
(1849-1890), Grand Duke of
Luxembourg (1849-1890).
As William died without male heirs,
Luxembourg fell to a collateral
branch of the Nassau family

Wilhelmina (1880-1962),
Queen of the Netherlands (1890-1948)

Juliana (1909-2004),
Queen of the Netherlands (1948-1980)

Beatrix (1938-),
Queen of the Netherlands (1980-2013)

William-Alexander (1967-)
King of the Netherlands (2013-)

Catharina-Amalia (2003-),
heir to the throne

first line Orange Nassau
Nassau Frisian line
second line Orange Nassau

Colophon

Abbreviations:

GAA	Gemeentearchief Amsterdam
AM	Amsterdam Museum
RMA	Rijksmuseum Amsterdam
KB	Koninklijke Bibliotheek
RMO	Rijksmuseum van Oudheden Leiden
RVD	Rijksvoorlichtingsdienst Den Haag

2017 Twelth edition
© Bekking & Blitz Uitgevers b.v.
Postbus 286
3800 AG Amersfoort
The Netherlands

ISBN 978 90 6109 4845

Cover
View of Delft, Johannes Vermeer
(1632–1675)
Mauritshuis Den Haag

Graphic design
Marieke Deij-Bausch
Gerdy Seegers